FINANCIAL
FOTOGRAPHS

How to Talk to Your Family About Money

KEVIN GEBERT

WINNIPEG, MANITOBA, CANADA

KNOWLEDGE BUREAU NEWSBOOKS

Kevin Gebert

FINANCIAL FOTOGRAPHS
How to Talk to Your Family About Money

Printed and bound in Canada

Library and Archives Canada Cataloguing in Publication

Gebert, Kevin, 1972-, author
    Financial fotographs : how to talk to your family about money / Kevin Gebert.

Includes index.
ISBN 978-1-927495-15-5 (pbk.)

    1. Finance, Personal--Canada. I. Title.

HG179.G42 2013   332.02400971   C2013-906615-2

Published by:
Knowledge Bureau, Inc.
187 St. Mary's Road, Winnipeg, Manitoba Canada R2H 1J2
204-953-4769
Email: reception@knowledgebureau.com

Publisher: Evelyn Jacks
Editors: Nicole Chartrand and Jaime Kyle
Cover Design and Layout: Evelyn Jacks and Carly Thompson
Page Design and layout: Karen Armstrong Graphic Design

Table of Contents

Part 2: Financial Planning Processes

Part 3: Preparing for Life's Financial Events

Part 4: The Next Conversation

Acknowledgements

With the amount of hours I have spent in my financial planning studies, it is easy to take pen to paper or keyboard to screen and create pages with important financial planning information for others to read. But writing a book is a whole different story, not just the words on the paper but the genesis behind the reason I am here today and the path that I took to get here.

I never knew that a move to Winnipeg, Manitoba in the early 1990's would set the plan in place to become a financial planner. For if it wasn't for an introduction to Timothy Kennedy by Rev. Jeff Anderson I may not be a financial planner today. Thanks Tim and Jeff!

In 1995, looking for a license sponsor, I found a name in the yellow pages with the biggest font and gave him a call. I would like to thank the late Harold T. Hope for giving a young guy a chance in the investment world.

I would like to thank my 3 biggest supporters who have given me the time I needed to complete this book; my wife Wendy, who is a wonderful educator, my son Preston, who is my writing partner and a future author, and my daughter Elayna, who always has a smile when daddy needs one.

My grandparent's Joseph and Hazel Gebert have seen my financial planning business grow from day one and have been a great support in listening to my many stories about my business and the book over the years and because of a 30th birthday gift, they gave me the idea of this book that has finally been born.

To my parent's Len and Louise Gebert for their willingness to be part of this book, as it is my 41+ years as their son that built the theme of this book.

A special thanks to the great people at the Knowledge Bureau who have worked many hours to produce this book and to give opportunity to a new author to write. Evelyn Jacks, Alan Gordon, Nicole Chartrand and Jaime Kyle - you are all just wonderful people to work with.

Thanks to Michelle Kilty for your continued financial planning support over the years.

To my first client, Lee Marshall and every client to follow, thanks for giving me the opportunity to become a small part in your life as we work together to build your unique financial plan.

CHAPTER 1

Just Coffee

Coffee, n. break fluid - **Anon**

Initiating
Conversations

> *What is a vivid memory you have of your childhood that illustrates your parents' financial status during that time?*
>
> *What word or words were used the most when you were growing up that told you that your parents' finances were good or not so good?*
>
> *What is one lesson you wish your mom or dad would have taught you in regards to finances?*

Why do you do what you do? Are you ever asked this question by family and friends? It may be an odd question to some, but the answer I would give is a cup of coffee. A small cup of coffee from our local McDonald's on 'Payday Friday' in the 1980s. I was not the one drinking the coffee, as I didn't find this caffeine craving until my Grade 12 graduation. It was my dad who had the only cup at the table.

How pivotal a cup of coffee can have on a person's career choice is anyone's guess. The funny thing is that I didn't put my 'why' together until many years after, my first client, Lee, signed all the new client forms.

The closest our family got to talking about money when I was growing up was speaking the common phrase: "we are living paycheque to paycheque."

"We are living paycheque to paycheque."

As I grew up there was always enough food on the table, plenty of gifts under the tree, a new pair of soccer cleats each fall, and a way for me to attend my out-of-town soccer games and tournaments that my parents couldn't afford to attend.

1

At my dad's 60th birthday party, my brother Darren reflected on what it was like having a great man as our father growing up. He recalled something that brought many tears to my eyes and still does to this day. The recollection was a story of our parents taking us out to McDonald's on most 'Payday Fridays' for dinner and my dad often just having a cup of coffee with the excuse that he wasn't hungry. As kids we didn't think much of it as we hunkered down on a burger, fries, and pop which were always followed by dessert! But to my dad, he thought that there were other pressing issues that needed attention with the few dollars it would have cost for his meal and that he could always get a bite to eat at home from my mom's great cooking! He had more enjoyment seeing his hard work as a carpenter provide a simple meal for his family with his cup of coffee in hand than enjoying a burger and fries himself.

"My parents made sure that we would be able to attend our long distance sports trips but we always caught a ride with a teammate."

A conversation over coffee is a common theme in my business whether it is at my office, at a client's home, or at a local Tim Hortons or Starbucks. As I listen to the story of the person sitting across from me, I usually answer questions through the use of pictures explaining how I may be able to assist. By drawing on a piece of paper or by 'painting' a picture through our conversations, I am able to explain my thoughts in simple detail. I find this approach an easier way to make the first attempt at an explanation on financial planning issues rather than referring to the 'textbook' answer all the time. I then back up my thoughts with theory and other resources at future meetings.

The pictures I draw are far from a 'Picasso or a (Art) Garfunkel,' as the Barenaked Ladies sing. My reason for drawing is to introduce financial planning concepts that could result in solutions without using the textbook answer. Simple explanations create a comfort level with the decisions that need to be made. If there is no attempt at building financial planning knowledge, decisions won't be made and in the end, I have not done my job.

So you may ask why I do what I do. The answer is because I want a country of people that are better educated in the area of financial planning than I was. Because I love being even a small piece in the goals and dreams my clients achieve from the financial planning work we do together. And maybe most importantly, because I want everyone to have a financial plan in place so they don't have to be someone's dad, mom, or other family member and only have a cup of coffee because they are looking after their family first and their personal needs second because the budget is just not there.

Creating a budget as a family

So the next time you're with family or friends having a cup of coffee, tea, or hot chocolate, pose a question about investments, budgeting, retirement planning, or money in general, and see where the conversation goes. It may be a short conversation, the person you're with could change the conversation to another subject, or maybe you'll spend the next hour learning something from someone else and in turn continue to build your financial planning knowledge.

Sharper Focus

1. Create a family budget with your children (or your parents, or your roommates).

2. Help your kids understand the value of money

    a. Take your kids to the bank to deposit their money and explain why it's important to save and the benefits.

    b. Teach your kids to make financial decisions ("You can buy the chocolate bar or save your money for a new video game.")

CHAPTER 2

Picture Time

To take photographs means to recognize—simultaneously and within a fraction of a second—both the fact itself and the rigorous organization of visually perceived forms that give it meaning. It is putting one's head, one's eye and one's heart on the same axis. - **Henri Cartier-Bresson**

Initiating Conversations

What is one picture that you will be sure to show your children when they are older?

What is one picture that you wish you had in your album but don't?

What picture is the most valuable to you?

When I was young I was a true pain in the —you know where—when it came to family pictures. I just did not see the benefit of so many 'takes' just to get the right look. To think that I would ever have to apologize to my mom in such a public way and say thanks was something that never crossed my mind until I started writing this book. And Mom, I stand on the highest mountain to tell everyone who can hear - I am sorry! Some people just don't get my humor, right Mom?

My first paycheque at McDonald's

Growing up I always knew what time it was when we had a family gathering or another event big or small. It was 'picture time'. I hated having my picture taken again and again just in case I shut my eyes or even dared to make a funny face. I even went to great lengths one year and got a buzz cut the day before a family picture. That did not go over well! Where were digital cameras in those days? If only I knew about *compounding interest* rather than *compounding pictures*, I could have saved my parents a few dollars once in a while. We always joked as a family that my mom must have made the photo shop rich with her business alone—maybe even twice or three times as rich due

Family trip to Disneyland to the doubles and triples that were always ordered and stored away for future reference. What I didn't know was that some of the photographs would be for my benefit years later. To this very day when a camera goes off I can't help but ask, "Are you sure you don't want to take another one?" Or, I just keep a never-ending smile on my face, in a joking way of course. Or, maybe not.

It's amazing how two events can change the way I will forever look at a picture again. The first event was a birthday gift from my grandparents and the other was the birth of my son, Preston.

It was my 30th birthday and my wife, Wendy, had organized a small birthday party for me as it was very important for her to celebrate this event as I was first to turn 30. Or maybe it was just a dry run to show me how to help her mom with her 30th birthday 121 days later. Either way, I would have just as well passed it off as just another day or maybe wait to celebrate once I was over the hill at 40.

After "Happy Birthday" was sung and the candles were blown out (yes every last one!), I was given a present from my grandparents. The gift was an album with a picture of my grandma all smiles sitting on a couch with me. I must have been 13 years old or so with a great 'non' hairstyle! As I opened the album and looked through it, tears filled my eyes as I realized what kind of priceless gift this was. I guess you are never too old to cry. At least they were happy tears!

The album started with a picture of my grandparents' wedding day with my grandpa sporting a moustache I wish I could grow. Also included were pictures of my years growing up, my first haircut, first tooth lost, and ended with a picture of my wedding day with my beautiful bride, Wendy. You are never too big to give your grandma a hug so I did, once my tears were wiped away.

I often look through this album to take some time from a busy day and remember the many events throughout my life.

As the birth of my son, Preston, was fast approaching I was thinking of something special that I could give him as he got older. Being a sports nut I thought of annual hockey card collections. Remembering my childhood when I took Wayne Gretzky rookie cards and attached them to the spokes on my bike. If I only knew what kind of financial mistake that would be. I should have kept them all in mint condition. At least we have one 'near mint' number 99 rookie card in the family. I am sure my brother would say he owns 51% of The Great One.

My wedding day

I remember visiting my grandparents as a child for family gatherings and viewing a slide show of pictures a number of times. So, I decided that it would be a great idea to buy a camcorder to capture my son as he grows up so that he would have both video and pictures of his childhood when he gets older. He can't stop smiling and is okay with pictures so far. I am sure by the time he is in his adult years everything will be in 3D.

Why do I talk about pictures? It has turned out to be my way to teach others about the importance of financial planning. As a financial planner I work with people from all walks of life, looking at the 'financial pictures' of their lives that are great, but at times may need a re-take or two. Everyone wants that perfect picture, but it is usually hard to get. Taking a picture helps us remember a specific time or event in our lives.

If you were to develop your own financial planning album what would the pictures look like? Would you want to skip over a few pictures that you wish that you could have re-taken?

Is there something you wish you would have experienced in the past but didn't, so there is no picture available? A trip you were hoping to take but decided it was best to save your money instead? A financial decision made that was hard at the time?

Do you have a picture of graduating with your university degree? How many hours did you put into your accomplishment? It could have been for personal achievement or to have a better opportunity at a career of your choosing.

Do you have a picture of your first cheque from your first job? It maybe wasn't worth much, but it most likely taught you spending and saving habits without you even realizing it at that time.

Do you recall a picture that your parents may have taken of you studying during high school? Maybe it was reminding you of your dedication to your studies that enabled you to receive a scholarship that saved your parents a few dollars of tuition money and building your future at the same time.

Do you have a picture from a car show that you attended? A great example of money management because of the money it costs to re-model a collector's car.

The pictures that you will see in *Financial Fotographs* are meant to help you insert a similar example from your life to make the chapter as personal as possible. Personal in a way, that will best relate the specific financial planning topic to your unique situation.

Sharper

Focus

- Talk with your friends and family about the financial pictures in your lives.
- What financial pictures do you wish you had?
- What financial re-takes would you do?
- What financial pictures do you treasure?

CHAPTER 3

On the Buses

All I ever wanted to do was write songs and get on a bus and go play them for people. **Chely Wright**

Initiating
Conversations

Have you been able to accomplish an important goal that you have been working towards?

Did you let obstacles get in the way of accomplishing a goal?

Is there anything that you would have done differently to meet a goal knowing what you know now?

When I was growing up I often heard laughter coming from the family living room. The source: my parents laughing to the show On the Buses which was a BBC show broadcast on the local PBS station, if I remember correctly. I didn't get the humor, but as long as my parents were enjoying the show, all the better! Not many people get the humor of Mr. Bean either, but he makes me laugh.

'On the buses' was how I spent most of my early years in the financial world. Laughter was something that I did not want to experience if the people I was meeting found out how I got to their home or the coffee shop for our initial meeting. I had to take the chance because I was determined to succeed in the competitive world of finance and I was jumping in with both feet running as fast as I could. My wife, Wendy, had a red sports car and therefore was my taxi service, picking me up after meetings when she could. I especially appreciated this if it was raining.

"Yes. I get to do what I am passionate about as my job."

I had worked for a year selling shoes and sports apparel to save enough to survive the first year of my new career. Not the wisest move at the time to some, but to my first client, Lee, and to the others that followed

"No. Took the bus. Now I drive." they must have seen my ambition for them to take a chance on the new guy.

Since I wasn't lucky enough to have someone in the business to take over from in the future and I didn't want to work at a bank, my first few months on the job were adventurous to say the least. A lot of snow fell in my first RSP season which caused the cancellation of many meetings, and it was more enjoyable traveling on the bus when it was not raining or snowing.

My business was slow to grow in the beginning. I am sure there were those who I met that just didn't want to invest with a financial advisor in his early 20s who couldn't even afford a car. You can't say the effort on my part wasn't there though.

I always wanted to become the type of advisor I would want to have if I was the prospect or client. I was lucky to have income as an advisor assistant and was able to take time to study and fulfill the educational requirements I needed to qualify to write the Certified Financial Planners designation qualification exam. Although the term "financial planner" wasn't well known at the time, I felt that this would be important to take for the future. Walking out of the six-hour exam that Saturday afternoon I was totally exhausted, but in the end it was well worth all those hours of studying as I was sent the approval letter in the mail a couple of months later. No online exam marking during the late 90s!

Since the beginning of my career I have continued to upgrade and look at areas of study where my clients need that expert advice. I like the fact that I have decided to be a general financial planner and surround myself with other professionals that I can refer to as a client's situation warrants. A promise I make to my clients is that if I don't know the answer, I will find it. One of the programs I am involved with is *The Family Office of Financial Planning Conversations.* Here we have a group of professionals with a diversified skill base that can be a resource within a client's unique financial plan depending on the scope of the need.

I chose to become a financial planner and had many hurdles to jump to bring myself and my practice to where it is today. What hurdles have you had to jump to get to where you are today? Are there hurdles that you just couldn't jump and therefore you settled for another career? Are there hurdles that you know you need to jump regardless and have just put them off?

One lesson that everyone should know when a specific career choice is made is that you need to be financially sound whether you are an entrepreneur or an employee. You may be just thankful at the beginning that

Made more cold calls.

you have a job or are able to start a new career, but soon thereafter you need to find a financial planner to set a roadmap in place to take care of your financial well-being. *Financial Fotographs* is a book that will hopefully plant some seeds in your financial planning and start the growth of important conversations you should have along the way to find out how you will define your own financial freedom. Make sure you utilize the additional web resources that are available at www.financialfotographs.com.

Sharper Focus

- Don't let hurdles get in the way of your passion.
- Talk with your family about what your financial goals are and discuss what you can do to overcome obstacles. Think about simple things like:
- No cable television for the summer.
- Ride your bicycle or take the bus.
- Eat out less.
- Ask your family and friends what sacrifices they took to get to where they are today.
- If you had it all over to do again would you have made a different choice with your chosen career?

CHAPTER 4

Red Card? Not Me, Referee! – 'Financially Speaking'

Of the nine red cards this season we probably deserved half of them. – **Arsene Wenger**

Initiating
Conversations

Did your parents talk to you about money? If so, how did they approach the subject?

When is the right time to start talking about money with your kids?

Was there a time that talking about finances backfired?

I played soccer for most of my childhood and even had the opportunity to play in the Canadian Championships in my grade 8 year, which was a great experience. I was an aggressive player, but never got my name in the referee's book until a men's league game many years later when I received a yellow card for what I would say was a fair tackle. I guess I can be happy to say that I never received a red card, although there were a few times in my soccer career in which I bit my tongue as my words could have led to a red card or two had I voiced my 'correct' interpretation of the call to the referee.

"Yes but just a bit. "Paycheque to paycheque' were the words often used."

It wasn't until I started studying for my first licensing exam that I wished my family had talked more about finances when I was growing up. There was no 'red card' to be given out because it really wasn't a topic that my family engaged in. On the other hand, we were never told that we couldn't talk about money. What we knew was that things were tight and that my parents lived paycheque to paycheque. That was it. Enough said.

My wife and I have always talked about money. Sometimes too much from my point of view, but it has always worked in both of our favours to know where we are at financially. This wasn't the easiest thing to talk about early on in our marriage, as my financial planning practice was really not

> *"As soon as they start putting money into their very first piggy bank."*

established yet and my wife was going back to school to get her education degree. But we did talk about it, and I am sure it prevented us both from making money mistakes. Outside of client meetings I am often in a marketing mindset and it is easy to spend more money on promotional activities than you take in and forget about your financial responsibilities at home.

Outside of my work as a financial planner, I really don't have many conversations about money unless someone else initiates the conversation. Not because I don't want to be seen as 'prospecting the masses,' but because it really doesn't come up unless I am having a business conversation with a client or prospect. With the growth of social media, I am finding that the subject of money, debt, and financial planning is becoming more common, and that is great to see. Sparking conversations about money is the reason for this book!

In his novel *Insiders*, Marvin H. McIntyre writes, "Money is the last taboo. People will talk about their sex lives before they discuss their finances." Is this true? To some people, money is a personal issue of which they don't want to talk about. To others, comparing recent purchases is the topic du jour. What I would be thinking from my financial planning mind is whether the item was purchased with debt or if it is leased.

If you don't want to talk about money, how would you respond if someone you were talking to started to talk about debt? Maybe this is the new taboo. In North America, the debt level seems to be climbing with no resolution in sight other than passing the ever growing debt balance on to future generations to solve. It's time to talk about money and debt no matter how uncomfortable it may seem!

As a financial planner, my job is to talk about finances, and I often start the money conversation with debt balances rather than asset balances. My role is to assist in a client's ability to increase their net worth, and one important step is paying down debt as soon as possible and minimizing the need to use debt in the future.

I spent a few years presenting a program I called *Fun with Finances* to grade 10 and 11 students at a local high school, as I wanted to contribute to the money conversation at the high school level. I started talking about money with my son when he was three years old. I began the conversation with a simple but repeatable phrase, "no work, no money, no food, no clothes, no toys…" I think it stuck when my son went from saying, "Dad, don't go to work!" to "Dad go to work!" When should you start talking to your friends and family about money and debt? Now! When should you start talking to your kids about money and debt? As soon as you start putting your first nickel into their piggy bank!

Not that I can remember.

As a Canadian you are your own referee when it comes to finances and I would suspect that many would have a 'red' card in hand when someone, even remotely, struck up a conversation about money with them. I have often found that the best referee in any game is one who is not noticed at all. So, the goal of Financial Fotographs is to help Canadians put their 'red cards' away and make conversations about money a part of everyday conversation.

Sharper

Focus

- What 'red card' moments, if any, have you experienced when talking about money with your parents or other loved ones? Think of ways that you can approach the money conversation so that it is 'fair play.'

- Take a trip to your local bookstore with a friend and pick up a book on money and finances. Make a plan to discuss what you have read over a cup of coffee each week.

- If you are a parent, develop a few fun activities that will encourage a conversation about money with your children. Maybe a game of Monopoly®?

CHAPTER 5

Green, Amber, Red

Our character is basically a composite of our habits. Because they are consistent, often unconscious patterns, they constantly, daily, express our character. – **Stephen Covey**

Initiating
Conversations

What is one bad money habit that you have?

If you are married, what personal money habit became a shared value with your spouse?

What new money habit have you learned recently that has helped you in your overall financial plan?

Earning your driver's license doesn't mean you will be the best driver in the world. Nor does it guarantee that you will never get in an accident or receive a ticket during your driving lifetime. You need actual experience behind the wheel to instill the rules of the road and develop good and safe driving habits.

Impulse Buying

When you receive your first paycheque from your employer, it doesn't mean that you will have the best financial plan in the world. You need to learn how to use your earned income effectively so that you can do the best you can with what you have. The experience of having money and being responsible for your well-being will hopefully teach you financial lessons to live by and lessen the bumps in the road.

In his book, *The Seven Habits of Highly Effective People,* Stephen R. Covey defines a habit as an "intersection of **knowledge, skill** and **desire**.[1]" *Knowledge*, being what to do and why to do it, *skills* being how to do it, and *desire* of wanting to do it.

---

[1] http://boykepurnomo.staff.ugm.ac.id/wp-content/uploads/the-7-habits-ofhighly-effective-people.pdf

Just like traffic lights have three colours to follow, so do your financial planning habits.

Green – *What I Should Do*

You know that as you approach a green light when driving that it is your 'right of way.' When it comes to your financial plan, you need to develop the following 'green light' habits so that you get off to a great start and keep going in the right direction.

Budget – Knowing where your money goes is important to keep you out of debt. You need to develop a budget and keep track of everything that you receive as income and everything that you spend on a monthly basis. Once a few months pass, you will learn what your average spending habits are in different categories.

Family and Friends – You need to ask your financial planner how to run a budget. You should also consider asking your family and friends how they do it. You may find that not every method clicks with you, but I am sure that if you at least ask, you can learn a few valuable habits.

Credit – It's important to build up a positive credit history as it will benefit you in the future. Make sure you always pay off your credit balances in full each month. A good habit is to pay for your necessities on credit and then transfer the exact amount of your purchases from your banking account directly to your credit card account once you get home. This is very easy and quick to do with today's technology.

Lifestyle – Develop a lifestyle that you can afford and be brave if this is different than your friends and family. You need to look out for yourself and your future.

Teach children – Money concepts are teachable from age three and beyond. The overall principles are the same, but the level of detail is obviously different depending on your children's ages. Teaching your children good money habits will put them on the right track and help them understand why you can't let them have everything that they want when they want it.

Work benefits – It is essential that you read and understand your work group benefits book. Not knowing what benefits you have can cost you more out of pocket expenses in the long term. Make sure you show your benefits plan to your financial planner so that the work plan can be part of, rather than separate from, your personal financial plan. It's equally important that you inform your planner if you have a group RSP, pension plan, or another savings vehicle at work.

Learn from past mistakes – You are not going to be perfect. There are going to be times that you are not going to follow your financial plan, or you may feel as though the hard work is not worth it in the long run. Make sure you learn from your mistakes so that they are not repeated when they would have really put you in a bind.

Knowledge is 'king' when it comes to financial planning. The more you know the better because you need to be involved if you are going to be successful. You don't need to know everything right away, but through reading, experience, and talking to your financial planner, family, and friends on a regular basis, you will be doing what you need to do.

Skills are learned and learning from others is a great habit to have. You should also to do some skill building on your own—try taking a course or reading a book on finances.

Desire is not given to you. You need to have a personal desire to succeed in your life to be able to implement your unique financial plan that will get you to where you want to be.

Amber – *Should I or Shouldn't I*

If you are close to the intersection when the light turns amber, you need to decide whether you have time to drive through the intersection or if it is best to stop. There are many decisions that need to be made in financial planning, as situations change all the time.

Risk – We will explore risk in a later chapter as everyone tends to view risk in their own way. From an investment perspective risk, can be defined as the willingness of an investor to weigh the risk of losing money over the potential of an investment gain over a period of time. The more potential for a gain also has a similar or more potential of a loss. If I was to ask a group of people what the definition of risk means, I would likely receive a different answer from each person. There is nothing wrong with this, but it is important to understand what risk means to you so that you know if you should take more risk or not.

Spending too much – It should be obvious to you that spending more than you earn creates a problem. You may want to spend more one month, but you need to balance that overspending by spending less the

You need to work hard for what you earn.

month following. This may seem simple, but unless you keep track of your spending habits, you may run into trouble sooner than you think. If you find yourself on the fence about whether you should buy something 'not on the list', that's usually a good sign that you should not go ahead with the purchase at the current moment, but instead plan for it in the future.

Eating out too much – It is amazing how easy it is to get lured into eating out often—because everyone at work is going for lunch, or you want to meet up with friends on the weekend, or you don't feel like cooking, etc. Encourage your friends and family to visit you at your home or have a potluck to cut down on the costs of eating out. Buying in bulk might not look 'cool' but it is 'cool' when it comes to keeping to a food cost budget. I am not saying to never eat out again, but rather create a healthy habit of what you eat and when you eat out.

Buying a house – If you can afford it, you should buy a house. The question of what kind of house is the answer that you need to find. The answer is not always the one you will be looking for either. A principal residence is one of the biggest tax free investments that the Canadian government gives us, but timing is everything. You want to make sure that you will be able to afford your home each time your mortgage comes up for renewal. There is nothing wrong with starting small and building from there, but you never want to be a home owner for only the length of your first mortgage and then go back to being a renter.

Buying a vehicle – I know the importance of having a vehicle as I did take the bus for the first few years of my career. The question you need to answer is: "should I buy this vehicle or should I buy that vehicle?" Personal preference is important, but being budget conscious is also critical in this purchase. You may need to re-look at your budget to be able to fit a vehicle purchase in as this purchase might spread over five years if you don't have the money saved up.

Only one partner handling the couple's money – This could create friction in any relationship if both partners want to handle the pocket book. The best way to settle this issue is to have a monthly family meeting to go over the books and learn from the previous month. This will ensure that things don't get out of hand and avoid having one partner be too embarrassed to tell the other that the books don't look good or worse yet, let it ride for a number of months just to avoid the conversation all together. Therefore, the question of "should you or shouldn't you" is answered by determining what is best for your personal situation. You can create an experiment where both partners take different roles before you decide on one person being the boss or both partners taking on the responsibility together.

Set goals and reward yourself – Setting a reward if you meet a budget, savings, or debt repayment goal is a great thing to do. You should reward yourself for meeting your goals, but you shouldn't do this every time as a 'reward' section on your budget is not going to pass every month.

Knowledge is only good if you want to learn. You need to find the depth of learning that you feel comfortable with at the beginning and build from there. You may like to have the 'Coles Notes' of financial planning knowledge, but in depth knowledge will always benefit you more.

Skills are developed from experience and learning. Financial planning knowledge will help you in the skills department, but learning from others is just as important.

If you have no *desire* to learn about financial planning, then knowledge and skill development will be of no value to you. Often desire is based on ultimate necessity or seeing benefits from previous actions, so keeping your desire in a process that is not always enjoyable is necessary to meet your financial planning goals that you set for yourself and your family.

Red – *I Should Not Do*

If you see a red light up ahead, you know that you need to be ready to stop until it turns green and the intersection is clear to proceed. Waiting until the light turns green could be similar to waiting on a decision that you know won't fit into your financial plan at the moment. You don't proceed with what you want to do or accomplish until your plan allows it.

Risk – You should not take more financial risk than you can handle; however you may consider taking more risk if you are behind on your financial planning goals but this is not a good idea without understanding that this may put you further behind. You may decide to adjust your financial goals, or you could search for ways to re-write your budget so that you can risk investing more money to hopefully meet your goals. Consulting with your financial planner and further educating yourself in financial risk could improve your comfort level. Don't take on a level of risk that leaves you feeling unsettled.

Spending too much – There is nothing wrong with treating yourself or family on occasion, but don't make it a regular occurrence and a regular expense. Outside of the variable expenses on treats, if you are spending too much each and every month then you may be living outside a realistic standard of living. If you continue to spend too much, then there is most likely no desire to commit to a budget or you may have the mindset that things will be fine in the future.

Impulse buying – If the item and price is too good to be true then it might not be for you—that is, if you can't afford it. Make sure that you sleep on it and when you wake up the next day refer to your budget to see if there is a fit. If there isn't a fit you could always look ahead a few months to see what this purchase can replace in your budget. If a one-time purchase is that important, you will need to sacrifice elsewhere rather than putting it on your credit card. Planning purchases ahead of time will save you money in the long run because you can make sure the item is necessary before you go back to the store.

Holidays not on debt – If you are going on a holiday, make sure it is paid for prior to your arrival date. If you do this you can enjoy the holiday and not have to either worry about how you are going to pay for it during the trip. If you arrive back home having to work and pay the vacation debt off as quickly as possible to save yourself from high interest credit that you bought the trip on, the trip will not be as enjoyable as you deserve.

Having too many credit cards – Getting something for free (credit card application gifts) is fun, but often there are consequences that you don't factor in. You should know that each time you apply for credit your credit history is checked. This can become a credit score issue if you get your credit history checked too many times within a certain timeframe. Also, the more credit cards you have, the more difficult it might be to apply for additional loans. If you have multiple credit cards that are active and you don't *Pay the minimum of your credit card the day you receive your statement. Then set an alarm on your computer three days before the due date so that the balance is paid on time.* use them (i.e. only got them for the free gift) the next potential lender may assume that you have maxed out your credit on all active cards even though your balance may be $0.

Forgetting about retirement – Living in the moment is fine, but don't do it in lieu of planning for retirement. Whether you're in your 20s or in your 40s, the practice of saving for retirement is an important habit. With a tight budget, you may feel it's difficult to justify putting money aside for the future, but any amount that you can afford to put in a RSP or other investment will help. Once you reach the age of retirement, I am sure you would prefer to still be working because you want to rather than because you have to.

Relying on a possible inheritance – If you are lucky enough to receive an inheritance from a family member or friend, be thankful for it at the time, but don't include the possibility of it into your financial plan before it is received. People are living longer and decisions can be changed, so never rely on something that may not turn up as planned.

Don't increase your standard of living just because you received a raise or bonus – We all love being rewarded with a raise or bonus from our boss, but receiving one doesn't guarantee that another will follow, so don't automatically increase your standard/cost of living. You may need to save an amount for a future one-time purchase or build up your emergency fund. Also, once inflation is taken into account, you might not have much of the raise or bonus left.

Knowledge will benefit you by understanding that what you want to do is not currently possible and that you need to wait until certain situations change. If you know that you don't have the *skills* necessary to proceed with a certain financial planning goal, then you will benefit from learning this skill in the future. Having the *desire* to stop and wait until the right time to achieve a goal or to know that you are just not cut out for your current financial plan is a benefit. Realizing that you need to develop a desire to follow a financial plan will only benefit you in the long run.

Sharper

Focus

- What are your Green, Amber, and Red financial habits? Write them out and use them as a guide in developing your financial plan.

- What financial knowledge do you have and what do you want to learn?

- What financial skill do you want to develop? Make a commitment to develop this knowledge and skill in the next six months.

CHAPTER 6

Run and Fail, Walk and Succeed: The Effects of Financial Decisions

The more alternatives, the more difficult the choice.
- Abbe' D'Allanival

> Initiating
> Conversations

> *Do you live for the moment and worry about the future when it happens?*
>
> *Is there a financial decision your parents made in the past that you will learn from?*
>
> *Is there a wise financial decision your parents made that you hope to repeat?*

One day my family travelled to Wal-Mart in search of hockey helmets for our upcoming family skating lessons. Being near the toy section, I thought that this might be a good teachable moment about money. Simple is better for a five year old. My son Preston and I went in search of what toys we could buy instead of the helmet for the same price. We found a few toys that he would have liked. I don't know how much of a lesson Preston learned, but one thing I did realize was that toys are much more desirable than a hockey helmet; however, the toys just wouldn't keep my son safe on skates.

I like to enjoy the moment, but like to sleep on financial decisions to understand the future impact.

Financial decisions are often more complicated when you are looking at bigger ticket items such as a car or a home, but quick decisions can often have a negative impact into the future if the correct decisions are not made. When making purchases (especially impulse ones), many people quickly pull out the credit card and often don't consider how much is already charged on the card for the upcoming statement. That's why I like to try and 'sleep' on any big purchase decisions to make sure that it's a must have and that I can afford it. The 'yes' decision later could give you as much satisfaction as it would in the impulse moment. On the other hand I am sure you have been in a high pressure sales presentation as my wife and I experienced one day.

Have you ever asked yourself if you 'should' buy something? Or alternatively, have you ever asked yourself if you 'should' return something that you had recently bought? Easier to buy than return, I am sure!

Here are some examples of situations for which financial decisions need to be made:

Emergency fund – Not having a source of money to use during emergencies is a financial decision that will create a need to use credit (create debt) to pay for something needed right away or if a source of income is lost for a period of time. The importance of emergency funds is discussed in the chapter called 'Wayne said it's going to rain again daddy.'

Variable expenses in your budget – If you spend too much on variable expenses during a month or two it may be more difficult to afford your fixed expenses during a particular month. Therefore, it's important to ensure that you monitor your variable expenses and ensure that your fixed expenses are always covered every month.

Buying the big TV *(the depreciating asset)* – Many people seem to covet a bigger TV than they already <u>have</u>. I have to admit that I have many times. Buying items that depreciate will often cost you more if you have to buy using credit. Unless the purchase is of an utmost need you must think about the value you will be getting out of the purchase in regards to purchase price vs. length of time used. Often with depreciating assets (TV, computer) you can usually get the same product for much cheaper or something better for the same price in the near future.

Vehicle – In a world of low interest rates and low financing costs, it is easy to go beyond your means when purchasing a vehicle. To most, this purchase should be a 'fixed expense' in your budget. You may tell yourself that you are going to buy the base model, but end up agreeing to a higher end model with lifetime tires thrown in as part of the 'amazing' deal. It is extremely important that you determine a vehicle cost you can afford (including upkeep and insurance) and include it in your budget as a fixed cost before you even step foot on any dealership lot. If you have a great negotiator, make sure to bring him or her along!

House – A house is probably going to result in the biggest debt that you will ever have during your lifetime. The lending institution will limit the amount of money it will lend you. What you can afford and what you are loaned are often two different numbers. Since your home is one of the biggest tax free investments that the government allows, it is important to decide on a budget plan that will keep you in your home so you aren't forced to sell once your first mortgage term comes up.

Work hard to pay off your mortgage.

Mortgage – The lower the interest rate is or the longer the amortization term is, the easier it is to afford a mortgage, but you need to put many 'what if' scenarios in your financial decisions. You never want to risk the possibility that you can't afford a switch from a variable rate to a fixed rate if the market or a changed life situation creates the need to switch. Although the capital gain on your home is tax free if it is your primary residence, you don't want to stretch yourself too thin if the mortgage plan goes against what you had planned.

Retiring early – Everyone would like to retire early, but for most, it's not possible unless some smart financial decisions are made early in life. You may decide that you won't travel as much during retirement if you retire early, or you will only be able to travel for a certain number of years after retirement due to having a finite amount of money for travel during retirement. Or you can decide to spend extra money during your working years, creating a need for you to work longer than you would like during normal retirement years.

Risk – Risk and investing often go hand in hand. Not enough risk could stop you from meeting your goals by not having your assets grow to what you need. Too much risk can create a need to work longer than you would like to make up for those years in which your investments lose more than you can handle.

Education – With a limited amount of investible assets, should you put off investing or putting money against your mortgage to either save for your children's education or to further your own education? These decisions could affect your ability to receive a promotion, retire early, or having enough money to put your children through school.

Having a child – From personal experience, having children is a fixed expense for obvious reasons, but costs are often under budgeted. Something always comes up that is needed and isn't planned for. Like what my parents did for me and my siblings, my goal is to give my children the best life possible so that they can do the same for their children in the future. Do you have enough money to be able to afford a child? Are you willing to make decisions about your current money habits and re-arrange your budget so that you can have children without going into debt?

My children can live at home for free as long as they are going to school full time.

How one decision can affect others (snowball effect) – You need to decide what is best for you and your family depending on your circumstances. Decisions that you make today could positively or negatively affect a decision that you may need to make later on due to the result of any current decisions you make.

When it comes to decision making, you may want to run and hope you don't fail (short term fix), but I would rather walk and have a better chance of succeeding (long term fix) in my decision making process.

Sharper Focus

- Ask a family member older than you how he or she made decisions at your age.

- If you know someone who has made a decision about a situation that you are currently contemplating, talk to them about his or her decision making process and if they would do anything different.

- When making your next financial decision, prepare a decision map of the pros and cons for each option, and consider how selecting each option will affect future decisions that you may need to make.

CHAPTER 7

Good Debt vs. Bad Debt

We all think we're going to get out of debt.
- **Louie Anderson**

Initiating
Conversations

How would you define good debt?

How would you define bad debt?

What is the biggest debt you will have in your lifetime?

Many people ask me, "Should I have debt?" After going over their unique situation, most times I won't say yes or no right away—instead, I often answer, "It depends." I will spend time explaining the fact that debt may work to their advantage. That may be hard to hear from a financial planner, but it is true as long as it is controlled and you don't go off track. When I explain debt to clients, I always use the illustration of *good* debt and *bad* debt.

Good debt is a loan for purchases you make or apply for that will get you ahead in life and will benefit you and your family. It may be a car loan so that you will have reliable transportation

Debt that is used to purchase something that will benefit you going forward.

to your job, or it could be money borrowed for tuition so you can get that degree you always wanted to establish your career with or get that promotion. The theory of taking on good debt to establish a goal is to make more money once you have accomplished your goal (new career or job promotion). Hopefully you will be able to pay the debt back and benefit from the experience for many years into the future by earning a higher income and having a higher standard of living.

From a financial planning viewpoint, I believe that *bad debt* is any purchase that is not necessary or will not get you ahead in life. This type of

Debt that is acquired for impulse purchases and other things you buy that will not benefit you over the long run. debt will get you in credit trouble and may lead to consolidated repayment agreements to lenders or even bankruptcy. It could be a trip that you know you can't afford and will take months to pay for after you return. It could also be paying extra money on an upper scale car with all the bells and whistles when the base model meets your needs.

The *biggest debt* that you will likely acquire in your lifetime will be a *mortgage* (a good debt). Unless you win the lottery, your mortgage payments will likely last for 18 to 25 years —potentially even longer if you come into financial hardship, consumer debt, or upgrade your home. As I mention in the chapter called, "Our Mortgage Plan", the amount that you qualify for doesn't always mean the amount that you should borrow for your home.

When qualifying for a mortgage you will find that lenders take into consideration two debt service ratios to see what they are willing to lend you: Gross Debt Service ratio (GDS) and the Total Debt Service ratio (TDS). These definitions are explained in more detail in the resource section of www.financialfotographs.com.

Should I borrow money? A quick answer would be "yes" but with further explanation. Borrowing for a RSP contribution is good if you are able to receive an effective tax break and are able to repay the loan within your budget and within a reasonable time so that the amount of interest paid on the loan is not close to the tax break you receive.

Borrowing for non-registered purposes could make the interest you pay on the loan tax-deductible. In my view it is more of a risk since the money owing is often only paid back after a longer period of time and is often an interest only expense (principal owed stays the same) to keep the interest charged on the amount borrowed tax deductible. Often the investments chosen are of a higher risk, and therefore you could find yourself in a situation where your loan balance owing is greater than the market value of the investment portfolio you established with your borrowed money. Or it could work to your benefit. It comes down to your risk tolerance and your overall financial goal of making the investment in the first place.

Should I get a co-signer when establishing a debt repayment plan? Depending on your situation, this may be an option, but I believe it should be the next to last option (the last option being bankruptcy). You have to remember that your co-signer is also taking on the risk of your debt, so you should be mindful that you don't do anything to negatively affect his or her credit rating. If you have to go this route, you should realize that you have a money management problem and need to learn valuable lessons from your money struggles so they will not be repeated in the future.

Your Mortgage.

Do you know how much debt you can handle? Many people would answer this question "yes" if it is asked during the emotional state of purchasing something they believe they need. Before any big purchase, I recommend that you 'sleep on it'—if it is a great deal then it will be there the next day. Without establishing a debt management plan and a monthly cash flow plan, you will not know if you can afford the purchase or even if you should make the purchase. Some sales you come across are too good to be true. If you have trouble rationalizing a big purchase, then taking more time to decide will pay dividends for you in the future for other similar situations. There is nothing wrong with dreaming, but you have to remember that you eventually wake up in the morning from your dream to life and reality. I have yet to find a lender that will forgive a debt on a purchase when they hear, "I must have been dreaming when I purchased that TV." If you have found one, please let me know, but likely by the time you let me know, they won't be in business anymore.

Explaining debt to your children: Even as a financial planner, this is a hard conversation to have, as my family didn't use the word "debt" when I was growing up. It is a challenge for me with my kids, but I am having fun trying to create examples to share. The easiest one so far is our mortgage, as I often explain to my son that we have to work to pay off the loan from the bank. So yes, Mom and Dad do have to go to work. Or, we have to work so that he and his sister can have separate bedrooms and not have to share a room in a different house. He likes that, as Transformers and dolls just don't mix for a five-year-old boy. I believe that it is important to discuss personal lessons learned—good or bad—so that your children will learn what to do and what not to do when it's time for them to experience similar situations.

Even though you can buy a 'money tree' (Malabar chestnut or jade plant), money doesn't grow on trees... If your children don't learn about debt and expect everything to be bought for them, they may believe that indeed, 'money does grow on trees'. I'd even be coming by your home to look in your backyard for your 'money tree'.

Sharper

- Ask your friends about purchases that they wish they thought twice about before making in the past.

- Ask your parents how you reacted when you were a child and you thought money did grow on trees.

- Ask your parents how long it took them to pay off their mortgage or what circumstances created the reality of not paying of their mortgage yet.

CHAPTER 8

Could've, Would've, Should've

Hindsight is always twenty-twenty - **Billy Wilder (1906-2002)**

Initiating
Conversations

What is one important part of financial planning that you have learned in hindsight?

What is one lesson you did not learn from your parents that you are going to make sure your children know about?

What is one financial planning lesson that you are going to make sure your children learn at an early age?

In the early years of my career I remember considering a marketing idea from one of my suppliers. The idea was to buy each of my clients a lotto ticket and anticipate one of them winning the 'big one'. I would hope that the client who won would be nice enough to invest the winnings with me. Down deep I probably would wish that I would have kept the winning ticket. The marketing idea was pointing out the fact that it is highly unlikely that the lottery will fund your retirement. Many of us continue to wish and I guess there is nothing wrong with that.

It is better to know and say 'no' rather than wish that you would have known when it is too late to say' yes'.

There have been many times when I have checked my lotto ticket and wished that I *could've, would've, should've* added numbers 9, 13, and 37 to my other three numbers that were lucky enough to win me a 3 out of 6 winning 'free draw' ticket. Just think what six correct numbers could do for you? That's where hindsight comes in.

When you do proper planning you can only control the expected and hope to be ready for the unexpected. If you are going down the river in a canoe, you can expect to be dumped in the water at some point of your ride. If you have all the necessary tools—including a life jacket—

I wish I would have known what things cost, so that I would have learned the value of money.

you know that if you are dumped in the water, you will have a fighting chance to get back in your canoe or at least back to shore.

Hindsight shouldn't escape your financial planning, investment, or estate planning needs. It is very important to have your plan as 'hindsight proof' as possible.

Hindsight in the investment market: There will always be a time in the market when you will wish that you had bought an investment that your bragging neighbour bought because the return was higher than your investment pick. Sometimes, hindsight works to your favour when you are glad that you didn't do what that same neighbour did as you hear him cursing at a high decibel. His investment was supposed to hit a 'homerun' and be the ticket to an early retirement on the beach somewhere far from where he is now. He still sits on his lawn with his feet in the pool reading the stock charts to find the next possible gem.

Hindsight in financial planning: My goal when working with clients nearing their retirement years is that they will continue to work because they want to rather than because they have to. You don't base your investment returns on an unrealistic goal and spend the rest of your monthly income with no care in the world. There will be a time when you will wish you would have saved more. It makes sense to plan for less and hope for more even though you may need to work a couple of additional years longer than you had originally planned. Working longer because you didn't take undue risk is much easier to take than working because you made some unwise decisions years before. Enjoying your vacation without knowing that you will be paying for the trip when you get back home allows you to enjoy the trip the way you are supposed to. You can always work hard and play hard. When you work hard make sure that there is a financial plan so everything is paid for before you play hard.

Hindsight in insurance planning: In the movie *Forest Gump*, Tom Hanks sits on a park bench with a box of chocolates and says, "My momma always said, 'Life was like a box of chocolates. You never know what you're gonna get.'" You never plan to die too early, get sick, become disabled, or not be able to care for yourself. If something happens it is often too late to apply for the coverage you need. The longer you live, the more likely it is for you to be at risk of getting sick (morbidity) before dying (mortality).

Hindsight in tax planning: With tax planning software these days, it is much easier and quicker to prepare a tax return. Years ago when I completed my paper copy tax returns, I wish I would have paid more attention to the process because I am sure some deductions were missed.

> *Be thankful for what you have and that money does not grow on trees.*

Hindsight in debt planning: Having debt is not the best feeling in the world. Although debt is sometimes the necessary evil to get what you may need or want (house, car, etc.), it is wise to pay off your debt as soon as you can. The reason for this is that if your borrowing capacity is maxed out, you may not have the ability to have access to additional money when it is needed the most. You may feel great buying that new plasma HD TV over paying off your credit card balance, but the TV is not going to make you feel good if it's at the expense of losing out on something that is necessary to get you ahead in life or affording an immediate need. Remember that technology changes all the time and you will not get full value for your plasma HD TV in a fire sale.

Having a 'hindsight free' financial plan is not realistic, but if you maintain as much control as you can, then you are doing a great job. Being able to react in a positive way to events as they happen will make your financial plan as 'hindsight proof' as possible. If you don't plan, then there will be many times throughout your life when you will be doing a lot of wishing as opposed to living.

Building your financial knowledge will go a long way in winning the game of hindsight. Although this will take time, I believe it is time well spent. You will thank yourself in the future for spending the time to learn what it takes to make the necessary smart financial decisions and limit the problems caused when unfortunate events occur.

Sharper

Focus

- Take a piece of paper and put a line down the middle. Write down worst case scenarios on the left hand side with the consequences on the right hand side. After finishing the exercise are you ready for each possible consequence?

- What is an example of something that you bought and after a few weeks you wished you had not purchased it and could not return it?

- What plans are you going to put in place to have the best opportunity to continue to work during your chosen retirement years because you want to and if you were to quit on a particular day it wouldn't affect the rest of your retirement plan?

CHAPTER 9

Smile, But the Price Tag Needs to be Known

The purpose of our lives is to be happy. - **Dalai Lama**

Initiating
Conversations

> *Would you increase your standard of living if you received a raise or keep things status quo?*
>
> *Is it important to you to maintain your standard of living in retirement as you had during your working years?*
>
> *Do you think you have a better standard of living now than during your childhood?*

What were you listening to on the radio in September 1988? I am sure you heard the Bobby McFerrin song "Don't Worry, Be Happy" once or twice. Isn't this an example of what we want life to be like? An extra dose of happiness everyday and a limit to the worries of tomorrow?

> *I would keep status quo and put the raise into my savings.*

As a father I know that caring for two little ones is a responsibility that I cherish and work hard at even though every day is not easy with the busy-ness of life. My parents worked hard to provide a good standard of living for me and my siblings, and my goal is for my wife and I to do the same for our family. I can't remember the exact quote, but my father strongly recommended a few times when I was growing up that I should not follow in his footsteps of being a cabinet maker. I am sure that these words of wisdom were his way of trying to guide me to a better standard of living for me and my future family. Just an example of how wise my father is, as I don't think I could even hammer a nail straight into a two-by-four without hitting my thumb.

The words security, comfort, and joy are intertwined in the equation of establishing your standard of living, but there is always a reference to the amount of money it takes an individual or family to live on to meet their own definition of standard of living that is important to them. This amount of money can be determined by choice or by price tag. By choice (meaning you have the monetary resources) is always preferred, but the price tag (what the actual cost is) needs to be known.

Building a desired standard of living and maintaining it for as long as possible is always faced with the predicament of finding a balance between living for today (and how it will affect your life tomorrow) and planning for tomorrow (and how it will affect your life today). Is a balance in life possible without sacrificing today for tomorrow? Let's explore this further.

Living for today will bring joy for a period of 24 hours. Then what? Do you live like it reads on the back of a shampoo bottle? Wash, rinse and repeat? Do you know when to stop? If you only focus on today, everything you do is short-term based. You will always have to re-establish a long-term plan that will eventually become important to you for survival, as tomorrow will come whether you like it or not. Some people 'work hard and play hard' and that works for them very well (health willing), but it's always a good idea to budget for those activities that you can't do without, as well as for the occasional times to treat yourself and your family rather than always doing things on a whim. Living for today may even get bad enough where you will begin to start missing your monthly fixed costs because you begin to use the money set aside for these costs to pay for the fun today. So let's not go there!

Always *living for tomorrow* by sacrificing today will paint a picture of what you want your life to be like in the future and your daily life will likely not be enjoyable. You don't want to work so hard and not be able to at least enjoy a bit of the fruits of your labour because you fear the bills of tomorrow. Have you ever heard of someone working and saving everything for retirement and then they die a short time after the retirement papers are signed? I have.

> *Maintain my standard of living as long as I am healthy and can afford to.*

My goal is to give my family a better standard of living in which I can participate just as much.

What will your future look like if you don't plan for your retirement standard of living? When you are lucky enough to retire there are certain expenses that you hopefully don't have. For example, a mortgage payment, dependants still living at home, and a few other costs that were part of your working years. If you can live on 70% of your 'working income' during retirement that would be awesome. You may even want to calculate two different retirement standards of living. One for the early retirement years when you are more active and perhaps travel a bit. The other for the later retirement years when you may have to stay local and possibly have a few health issues you need to deal with. The more planning you can do, the better you will be, as you never know how long your retirement years are going to last.

If your financial plan can accommodate a standard of living for today, tomorrow, and into retirement that is reasonable, it is the ideal state to be in. This doesn't mean that it won't need to be adjusted many times over, because it most likely will as circumstances come up.

In a perfect world, you want to make the right financial choices (budget, limiting debt, investing wisely, keeping within your risk tolerance, and protecting your ability to earn money) throughout your life so that you can maintain a standard of living that you desire for you and your family for today, tomorrow and during retirement. If this can be achieved there will be more smiles going around and less looking at the price tag.

Sharper Focus

- Calculate what your retirement standard of living should be. Work with your financial planner on ways to achieve it.

- Look at your spending habits for the last 30 days. If these are impulse purchases what could you do to stop this from happening as frequently? Would you leave the credit or debit card at home and just bring enough money to buy what you need?

- Ask your parents how many times their standard of living changed due to circumstances, inflation, or personal choice.

CHAPTER 10

Riding the Emotional Rollercoaster

Cherish your own emotions and never undervalue them. -
Robert Henri (1865-1929)

Initiating
Conversations

Are you more emotional when you lose or when you win?

What experiences have you had along the 'emotional rollercoaster' with your past investments?

Does a bad experience increase or decrease your emotional reaction the next time?

Since 1958, the Playland Wooden Rollercoaster in Vancouver, British Columbia, has been a tourist attraction for many including myself a few times in my life. I even know a person who refuses to go on the ride out of total fear. I can't wait to take my daughter on it once she is both old enough and tall enough, as she has no fear.

I think a rollercoaster is a great illustration when it comes to talking about emotions that investors experience during every market cycle. The only difference is how each person can handle their different emotions in relation to their individual risk tolerance.

More emotional when I win; just mad when I lose.

The main difference between this old wooden rollercoaster and the stock market is that the rollercoaster is timed to end and then start again. A stock market cycle doesn't run for a fixed amount of time before it starts over again. If it was that simple, then it would be much easier to make money and we wouldn't have to worry about risk as much. Although stock market history is not guaranteed to repeat itself, there are many historical lessons that we can learn from to hopefully understand the stock market better in the future.

I often find that when things are great in the stock market, risk is not talked about. Investors are happy and enjoying the money that they are

Technology Bubble. Debt crisis. making (on paper) and thinking that the growth will never stop (and never re-allocate their assets). Eventually the time will come when uncomfortable volatility and a market correction appear and those same investors are wishing they would have cashed out sooner. Investors often forget why they invested in the first place and rather than riding things out, they cash out and swear to never invest again. That only lasts until the market regains its strength and things are starting to look like nothing could go

wrong again, but they often miss the best days to be in the market while they wait to get back in.

The cycle of market emotions illustrates that a full range of investor emotions can be broken down into three stages:

Stage One: The investor starts their investment cycle with *optimism* that the market will have a positive run for the next while. The emotion builds to *excitement, thrill,* and finally *euphoria* where the investor believes that everything is just going to be wonderful and they wish that they had more money to invest. What the investor doesn't understand is that they are at the **'point of maximum financial risk'**.

Stage Two: The investor has just enjoyed a great run, but was in no position to take the gains off the table and has just continued on as if nothing wrong could happen. But wait—something bad has happened in the market which has brought volatility to the front page of the news as analysts are saying that things are not going to look as good going forward. The same investor who has been on the ride up doesn't believe that things could get bad, but is anxious on hearing something negative in the investment news. As the negative news continues, there is increased volatility in the market and the gains once enjoyed are beginning to not look as good. As *anxiety* and *denial* creep into the investor's mind, they are still convinced that this will be a minor setback and that they are still in the market for the long-term. The market continues to become volatile as the negative news carries on, and companies are starting to come out with their quarterly reports. Some are not meeting analyst expectations, which also bring additional volatility to the market. Now *fear, desperation* and *panic* start to settle in and the investor is now wondering if all is lost and they should 'cut their losses' and run. They may even think that guaranteed investment certificates (GIC's) should be their investment of choice even though they vowed to never invest in anything like that. As the next quarter hits more companies are coming out with lower gains and not meeting expectations so the investors who are still invested experience *capitulation, despondency* and finally *depression* and just run and hide. What the investor doesn't understand is that this is usually the **'point of maximum financial opportunity'**. Most of the investors who are going to cash out have already done so.

Stage Three: It seems as though the bad news is starting to dissipate and *hope* is now being talked about in the marketplace. After a market quarter of higher than expected reports from companies, there is a feeling of *relief* in the market and eventually there is a feeling of *optimism* again. All investors that have stayed in the market are glad that they 'weathered the storm', and those that cashed out are most likely still licking their wounds and fearful of when the bottom will fall out again. Those same investors are often missing out on the best time to get back into the market due to the emotional rollercoaster they just experienced.

This ride on the stock market rollercoaster can last a long time at different emotional stages, but it is up to your financial planner to calm your emotional state when it comes to investing. If there is an appropriate risk tolerance developed at the beginning of your investment timeline and regular re-balancing of the investment portfolio is done, the volatility can be controlled better than just letting it ride. A market cycle is often 4-5 years, but the volatility of the cycle can be very volatile at times. Therefore, this is

It teaches you lessons about making better decisions next time. You will have a different response when you actually experience something rather than just reading about it.

a great time to reflect on the original reasons why you invested in the beginning. If your investment objectives do change enough where you believe that your current portfolio won't meet your investment and financial planning goals and objectives, then it is important to contact your financial planner to discuss.

Depending on your investment timeline, the risk that you experience in the market can have different responses. If you are near the beginning of your 'earning years', then the *anxiety, fear,* and *despondency* stages might not be as severe as an investor that might be closer to retirement or even in retirement. If you are investing on a monthly basis, you might even be encouraged by the volatility as it may be a great buying opportunity compared to someone who is drawing an income from investments during the same period and worried how much longer the same investment withdrawals will last.

In the end, each investor should know that investing in the stock market is a risk and how we interpret our reaction to this risk at each stage of the emotional rollercoaster is what we need to define sooner than later. Once we understand how we react to each stage, we can alter our financial plan accordingly and maintain it so that it will meet our goals and objectives with the least amount of alterations.

Information for this chapter was source from *Westcore Funds/Denver Investment Advisors* LLC, 1998.

Sharper

Focus

- Ask friends and family how they have reacted to different stock market events in the past.

- Write down what you will do with your investment portfolio if you experience negative stock market events in the future.

- Ask your friends and family what changes they have made in the past when uncomfortable market volatility strikes.

CHAPTER 11

Personalities and Money

I'm very confident in how I project my personality.

– Megan Fox

> Can you define yourself as one of the money personalities?
>
> What life events have changed your money personality?
>
> Do you see yourself taking on a different money personality as your lifestyle changes?

Initiating Conversations

As I recall my high school years, I would never have thought my personality would change as much as it has. I remember turning bright red and getting sweaty hands each time I had to talk to the class or make a presentation in front of my fellow students. I guess this would be true for many people in the same situation, but what I know now would have helped so much back then. As I have built my financial planning practice, I have become more and more confident in how I project my personality. My money personality has also changed along the way, as I have experienced different life events of being a business owner, buying my first home, and becoming a husband and father.

Have you ever thought about defining your money personality? In her book, *Your Money Personality: What It Is and How You Can Profit from It,* Dr. Kathleen Gurney, Ph. D. details her research on nine different money personalities. You may find that how

I see myself as part Entrepreneur and part Money Master.

you react to money situations strays away from your overall personality, or you may find your overall personality influences your spending, saving, and investment habits.

Dr. Gurney explains that a true sense of mental wealth is met when an individual meets the following criteria[1]:

Becoming a business owner, husband, father and buying my first home.

- You understand your money personality—how you relate to your money and how your attitudes affect your money behavior.

- You neither exaggerate nor deny the importance of money.

- Money is not viewed as an end in itself, but as a reward for achievement.

- You control your money instead of letting it control you.

- Money provides satisfaction and enjoyment as well as security.

I have found from experience that individuals tend to hang out with others of similar money personalities. It can be much different if you are bringing different money personalities into a romantic relationship. In the dating and marriage world, it can be said that opposites attract, but it is beneficial if a couple creates a new money personality together to make overall financial planning and investing smoother. If you are beginning a relationship with a new financial advisor, it is in the best interest of both advisor and client(s) to explore the different money personalities so the advisor can make sure that everything matches up or there are changes that need to be suggested.

Take some time to look through the following money personalities that Dr. Gurney presents in her book noted previously to see where you may fit in:

Entrepreneur
~ Don't view money as a primary motive but a result of hard work

Hunter
~ Like to rely on the advice of others to make easier decisions

---

[1] Pg. 397. Your Money Personality: What it is and how you can profit from it. Kathleen Gurney Ph. D. Financial Psychology Corporation. 2009.

High Roller

~ Money management creates anxiety and decisions are often impulsive

Safety Player

~ Concerned about protecting the money you have rather than increasing its value

Achiever

~ Desire to be involved and in control of money management can limit opportunities of growth

Perfectionist

~ Conservative risk tolerance

Money Master

~ Highly involved with money management

Producer

~ Financial anxiety makes it difficult to make decisions

Optimist

~ Don't like any stress caused by money

When I retire.

After finding your money personality, do you realize that you may have to make some changes to meet your financial planning goals? Would you feel more comfortable changing your money personality to meet your current financial plan or vice versa? Dr. Gurney says that "if you want to change your money style, you have to alter the internal ways you represent money—your personal financial traits—by changing negative attitudes and behaviours into positive ones."[2] You may learn more about your money personality by visiting www.kathleengurney. com where you may also purchase Dr. Gurney's book.

I challenge you to meet the definition of mental wealth and find the money personality that you are most comfortable with, as it will only help you in meeting your desired financial planning goals and dreams.

---

[2] Pg. 372. Your Money Personality: What it is and how you can profit from it. Kathleen Gurney Ph. D. Financial Psychology Corporation.

Sharper Focus

- Take a blank piece of paper and write down how you would define your money personality and how others might define it.

- Set goals to perfect your money personality.

- Ask and discuss with a parent or partner the differences between your thoughts and beliefs of money so that you all can discover what each of your money personalities are.

CHAPTER 12

Haircuts and Investment Styles

Style is what gives value and currency to thoughts.

– Arthur Schopenhauer (German Philosopher, 1788-1860)

Initiating
Conversations

Are you one to stick with your investment style or change to a style that is currently popular?

Would you be willing to try a new investment style if enough positive examples were presented to you?

Would you agree that investment styles seem to always return in the future?

Have you ever sat in the waiting area of your hair salon and thumbed through the hairstyle magazines ready to make a drastic style decision, only to decide when asked by your stylist that you would like the 'usual'? I have to admit that I do that every time only to stay with the 'business usual', keeping in mind what my clients would think if I got a more radical 'do. A harder decision is to either keep the grey or dye my hair. I am still not decided on that.

Investment styles are often reflective of the current market and future market trends.

I started getting my hair cut from Bev a few years into the start of my financial planning work and every time I go, I think about the small similarities of our two professions. Both Bev and I deal with styles. Maybe the investment styles are not as colourful as the various hairstyles Bev can offer, but they are important to review nonetheless.

An investment portfolio can contain a variety of investment styles. In the end though, your main focus should be to have an investment portfolio created for you that diversifies your risk but also creates a return potential that will meet your goals. Another aspect of style management is trying to create a portfolio where correlation (how investment return and risk differentiate from each other) creates an added risk and return benefit.

Investment styles that could be in your equity portfolio:

Sector Rotation – This investment style anticipates what the market trend may be and makes the appropriate portfolio re-balances. The re-balances could be for a certain time frame and could consist of an increase or decrease in the purchase of individual stocks. It could be a specific industry, size of the individual company stocks, or the amount of dividends received by a particular group of stocks.[1]

Fundamental – This investment style looks at a stock price by dividends, cash flow, sales and original cost rather than the size of the stock. When re-balancing, the profits from the stocks that are doing well are used to purchase more stocks that are not doing as well in the portfolio.[2]

Only if it will have a potential long term benefit.

Value – Investing with a value focus is where the port-folio manager looks for stocks that are undervalued or unpopular and are essentially 'on sale'. The manager or investor would be willing to wait for a long time for the stock to meet price targets that define the true value of the stock. A portfolio of value stocks tends to have lower turnover.[3]

Growth – A growth investor looks at the earnings of the individual stock and the potential of the price of the stock to increase in the near future compared to the overall market. A portfolio of growth stocks tends to have a higher turnover.[4]

---

[1]   14.18 – CSI Wealth Management Essentials vol 2

[2]   Invesco.ca

[3]   7.5 – CSI Portfolio Management Techniques

[4]   7.7 – CSI Portfolio Management Techniques

Momentum – This approach to investing is where the portfolio manager is looking at companies with the biggest stock price change in the recent months that they believe will continue higher over the next period of time. The downside of this option is that as stocks become popular, the price could be over-inflated and fall hard quickly, so you need to set a target of when to sell the stock.[5]

GARP (Growth at a Reasonable Price) – The portfolio manager uses a strategy that is a combination of both growth and value investment styles. An example of this style could be a stock that can be bought at a reasonable price and have great growth potential at the same time.[6]

Deep Value – An investment approach where a stock is defined as being highly undervalued and will need an even longer time to show its growth potential in its stock price. An investor may take an activist approach and look for management and structural changes in the particular company.[7]

> *The popular investment style could only last for a short time or it may be too late to change.*

Small Cap – An investment style where a portfolio manager will buy stocks within the definition of 'small cap', which is defined differently depending on if it is a Canadian stock, US stock, or global stock. These stocks tend to be more volatile and investors can experience high upside returns and deeper drops where the stock price could drop to $0.

SRI (Socially Responsible Investing) – An investment style where the portfolio manager uses a screening process that deletes all stocks that don't meet certain criteria. These criteria could be that the portfolio will have no companies that sell or produce tobacco, gambling, or alcohol.

---

[5] Investorama.com www.finance.yahoo.com Gaining Speed: Momentum Investing 16/4/10

[6] A guide to investment style page 2. Franklin Templeton Investments

[7] A guide to investment style page 2. Franklin Templeton Investments

Bond styles that could be in your fixed-income portfolio:

Real Return Bond – This type of bond is similar to a regular bond because it pays interest during the life of the bond term as well as the original principal at maturity. The difference is that both the interest payments and principal repayment are adjusted to inflation so that the investor will maintain their purchasing power.[8]

Corporate Bond – When investing in corporate bonds you are putting your faith in the strength of the individual company. Therefore, the potential interest rate that you would receive is most likely higher than a bond issued by the federal government. There is no guarantee (credit or default risk) of your interest and repayment of principal, but this is the risk you take for the potential higher interest rate received over the term of the bond.

Federal Government Bond – This is as close to a guarantee that you will get in the bond market, and therefore you are trading with the likelihood of receiving all interest and repayment of principal. The potential interest rate received will not be as high when compared to a corporate bond.

Laddered Bonds – This type of bond investing could be used when investing in corporate bonds or government bonds. The manager tries to spread out the risk of the overall portfolio by buying bonds with different maturity dates. For example, 5 corporate bonds are divided evenly between 1-year and 5-year maturities. When the 1-year bond matures, the money is used to buy a bond(s) with a 5-year maturity. The same process continues annually at maturity of the appropriate bond(s).[9]

Just like you would want a hairstyle that matches your personality, as an investor you want a portfolio that includes the necessary investment styles to meet your risk and return objectives.

---

[8] 15.14 - CSI Wealth Management Essentials vol 2

[9] investopedia.com

Sharper Focus

- During your next review meeting ask your financial planner what your current investment portfolio style is.

- Ask your parents or grandparents if they know what their investment style has been throughout their investing years.

- Look to your financial planner to show you how different investment styles have performed over the past 10 to 20 years.

CHAPTER 13

RDSPs

The message I'll share...is that inclusion is extremely important for kids with and without disabilities. - **Clay Aiken**

Initiating
Conversations

What is an important point to remember if you need money from your RDSP?

What types of investments can be included in a RDSP?

What is another government plan that would provide ideal assistance to a beneficiary without affecting any government benefits?

The wish of every parent is to see their child(ren) grow up and succeed in whatever they decide to do. I know this to be true firsthand as a father myself, even at this stage of life when my son wants to be an 'Angry Birds' expert and my daughter a princess.

The rules associated with withdrawals.

My sister and brother-in-law, Lisa and Sheldon, have the same dream for their five children, but with a twist. Their twin sons, Esra and Azriel, have Autism. They were diagnosed when they were young and each of them is brilliant in their own way. Esra loves to perform and Azriel is built like an offensive lineman. The twins deserve the best life possible and the Registered Disability Savings Plan (RDSP) enables them to build up assets to assist in their future financial security.

Paul Gauthier who is a Canadian Paralympic Gold Medalist also values the RDSP program. He says that 'The RDSP is a very progressive policy that government put in place to allow for security in the future for people with disabilities. This has been so exciting for families that are supporting their children and for adults with disabilities who worry about their financial footing. I chose to open an RDSP in hopes that I would be able to secure my future by saving money each month and by receiving the government grant, as well as being able to make wise investments with the money. This will help me be able to continue supporting myself and my family, after I am unable to work.'

The risk tolerance of the investments within a RDSP should be approached the same way as you would with any other investment. You need to choose a timeline to meet the length of time the money will be invested until it starts to be withdrawn. A risk tolerance will need to be defined so that the volatility of the investment portfolio can be controlled as much as possible. The portfolio should be reviewed regularly with your financial planner just like you would with any other investment portfolio (RRSP, RRIF, TFSA, etc.).

All eligible investments are included on an approved list that is available from your financial planner.

Tax free savings account

Although a government program can be changed at any time, the RDSP is a great plan that was created to assist in the future well-being for Esra, Azriel, Paul and other Canadians. The RDSP will provide extra monetary assistance to help with the extra financial burden family and friends could be faced with in the future depending on what is needed for each beneficiary and what the government at that time will provide

Sharper
Focus

- If you know of someone who qualifies for the disability tax credit make sure you tell them about the RDSP.
- If you are someone with a RDSP, make sure you set up a review meeting with your financial planner on a regular basis.
- If you are able to qualify for a RDSP make an appointment with a financial planner to review the benefits you can receive.

CHAPTER 14

TFSA vs. RSP: The Wrestling Match

Wrestling was like stand-up comedy for me.

– **Dwayne Johnson**

Initiating
Conversations

Should you have the same investment plan within your TFSA and RSP?

Should I max out my TFSA before I contribute to my permanent life insurance plan?

Should your mortgage rate or amortization be taken into consideration when deciding whether to put an extra amount against principal each year or contribute to your RSP?

I have to admit that I was a wrestling fan when I was younger up into my late 20s. On TV each week was the local show *All-Star Wrestling* along with the *World Wrestling Federation* (as it was originally called), which I recorded every weekend as it was on late. As the 'sport' grew (people have called it different things), I was drawn to the storylines and the characters of the 'squared circle'. Anyone remember the WWF cartoon series?

Each year many people have their own wrestling match. This time it is not Hulk Hogan vs. Dwayne "The Rock'" Johnson or "Macho Man" Randy Savage, but you vs. decisions for your financial plan. There are many decisions that need to be made so that your financial plan won't go down for the 1-2-3 count.

It all depends on your investment timeline and risk tolerance. If they are the same, then it might be a good idea to put the equities in your TFSA and the fixed income investments in your RSP.

One of the annual matches that you will participate in is the 'TFSA vs. RSP vs. Mortgage Pay-down vs. Other Debt' contest. In the end, it comes down to a conversation with your financial planner regarding tax savings vs. interest savings. The storyline could surround your current income levels, future income potential, investment

It depends on your situation, but it is good to compare liquidity needs, future growth potential, taxes payable, risk tolerance, and investment options prior to making the decision each year.

growth, and overall financial planning goals. Unlike wrestling entertainment matches, the financial planning decisions you make don't have a guaranteed or staged outcome.

Does your RSP account always win? It depends...

I don't know if every meteorologist would agree with me, but I believe that there are six seasons in Canada. Everyone should know the normal four. Can you guess what the other two are? Tax season and RSP season. From a financial planning perspective, RSPs should be considered throughout the whole year rather than just the first 60 days of each calendar year. It would even be nice if RSP contributions were due after taxes were submitted, but I don't see that happening anytime soon. Therefore, clients will often ask their financial planner if they should buy RSPs to save tax for the previous tax year or even 'top up' contributions that have already been made through their monthly contributions.

RSP contributions are a great way to save for your retirement, but the trick is to use them correctly. In a perfect world you should get a bigger tax break upon contribution and pay less tax upon withdrawal, but this is not a perfect science. I would argue that increasing your net worth is the main focus, and therefore crunching the numbers prior to RSP contributions is a valuable exercise each year.

Does your RSP account or the Mortgage Pay-down win? It depends...

Both goals are important, but you need to look further into this to be able to make the correct decision. Saving for retirement and paying down non-deductable debt is important. Have you figured out the mortgage interest savings of an extra $10,000 principal pay-down versus a $10,000 RSP contribution for the specific tax year? These calculations include a number of variables (marginal tax rate this year and in the future, length of mortgage term, projected investment returns, projected mortgage rates, allowable extra mortgage payments, etc.), but a general comparison is valuable as a start. Another option you may consider is to make the RSP contribution and contribute the tax savings to your mortgage when you get your Notice of Assessment back.

Will my TFSA or RSP win? It depends...

Financial planning consists of making recommendations before and during retirement to save clients from the 'claw-back' zone. A TFSA is a great way to do this. If you know that you are going to make more money in the future, it may be to your advantage to save your RSP contributions to a future tax year and contribute to a TFSA. If you are close to a projected claw-back, then you have to see if making RSP contributions will give you a net benefit upon withdrawal in the future. If your income level is going to be low for the remainder of your working years, foregoing RSP contributions and contributing the maximum yearly limit to your TFSA may be a good idea if you can afford it. If you are receiving government benefits, reviewing any claw-back issues is important to do prior to a RSP contribution as a TFSA contribution may be better for you. Always consult your financial planner prior to making a decision.

Will my RSP or my Other Debt win? It depends...

Most of the suggestions to this question are similar to the RSP vs. mortgage pay-down scenario because you are dealing with non-deductable debt (unless you have debt for an investment loan). Debt is a big problem in society and paying down debt is often the better decision even if it is just a good psychological feeling. Unless you invest your RSP in a guaranteed product, you are dealing with an uncertain future growth rate. You may have a line of credit, but the majority of debt is from credit cards and we all know how high those rates are. Ask your financial planner if it makes sense to hold off on RSP contributions and pay off additional debt.

Every year you may have a different part of your financial plan wearing the 'championship belt', but in the end, the decision should be made while considering the current state of your financial plan and what your financial plan could look like in the future based on your projections. It is up to you to write your own financial planning storyline with the best outcome possible; however, it is wise to look to your financial planner as the promoter of the best solutions from which you can choose.

It depends on how much interest you will save on your extra mortgage payment compared to the tax savings on a RSP contribution with the contribution amount being equal.

Sharper

Focus

- You have an extra $5,000 to contribute to either your RSP or mortgage this year. Ask your financial planner to compare the interest savings on your mortgage with a tax deduction from a RSP contribution.

- Ask your financial planner to show you what tax implications (when you withdraw money in retirement) you may have if you continue with the same annual contribution to your RSP until retirement. If you are not happy with the possible tax situation you may want to consider a TFSA contribution instead.

- Have your financial planner show you what your net worth could be in 10 years if you were to focus on paying down your mortgage rather than contributing extra money to your RSP and vice versa.

CHAPTER 15

What Should Be PACT in Your Financial Plan?

A big part of financial freedom is having your heart and mind free from worry about the what-ifs of life.

- Suze Orman

Initiating Conversations

> *What is your definition of protection when it comes to financial planning?*
>
> *When would someone who didn't have a financial plan wish that they had completed one?*
>
> *What would you do if you received an unexpected inheritance?*

The financial planning work I do with clients is not a product but a process. This process is one of the most important things we do together. Completing a financial plan and updating it on a regular basis will ensure my clients keep on the right path towards meeting their current and future financial planning and lifestyle goals. For you, retirement may be around the corner or not for another 25 years, but, right now is the best time to start your plan if you don't have one or to update it to make sure all the necessary changes are being made. I like to make sure I cover all aspects of a financial plan so that a client won't come back and say, "I wish I would have known that."

> *I want to make sure that I can protect my family's standard of living while I am alive if I can't work and preserve it if I predecease my wife.*

I like to use acronyms, as they are easy to remember. Therefore, I follow the financial planning process acronym **PACT**—**P**rotection, **A**ccumulation, **C**onversion, and **T**ransfer.

Many people believe that they are indestructible, and when an accident occurs they will wish that they had a financial plan in place in case of uncontrollable events to make as much of a smooth transition as possible.

The **protection** stage is the starting point for every financial plan so that you have a solid foundation to build upon. Having a few thousand dollars saved up for a 'what if' scenario may make you feel comfortable, but it will not help you if a major unfortunate situation occurs. *Life insurance* coverage is available to help cover your financial goals if you were to pass away. For example, it can be used to pay off your mortgage or make sure there is enough money to support your surviving spouse. *Critical illness insurance* helps you deal with the unfortunate scenario of you having a stroke, heart attack, or other illness by ensuring money is available to maintain a standard of living you are used to and providing the means to pay bills. *Disability insurance* is coverage that assists in paying the bills while you are off work due to a disability. Looking further into the future you may want a *long term care* plan that will provide coverage for care during your senior years so that your desired care is continued without the added expense passed on to your children. An *emergency fund* (rainy day fund) is not an insurance product, but a pool of money (3-5 times your monthly salary). If you don't have additional coverage for a particular situation that arises, your emergency fund should be fully accessible to help you through the emergency period.

The **accumulation** stage could include your RSP, Spousal RSP, Pension Plan, Tax Free Savings Account, or other investments or properties that you would like to see grow and use the proceeds during your retirement. It's very important that you establish your risk tolerance before you invest a nickel. The necessary evil of the stock market is volatility. It's the volatility that makes you rethink your investment objectives more often. It would be great if the market was always positive, but that is not realistic. You may want to plan for a 5% annual return and hope you get 8% so that you limit the surprises. It is better to plan for less and receive more than the other way around. If you take less risk, you may have to work longer than you originally planned, but it may give you a better feeling than needing to work longer because you took more risk than you are comfortable with and have to delay your retirement to make up the shortfall. You may end up doing some work during retirement, but it is better to continue to work because you want to rather than because you have to. When it comes to your pension plan at work, it is very important that you understand how it works as this will affect your retirement age, income decisions, and other investment decisions.

If I received one, I would try to spend it the way the one who passed would have wanted it spent.

Once you have decided to retire, you will be at the **conversion** stage. Hopefully your retirement decision is made years prior to the actual date so that you can create a smooth transition within your sources of retirement income. Pension decisions are made with your predictable future in mind, even though things can change. You will want to make sure that all sources of income (registered and non-registered) are received in the most tax-efficient way possible. You may want to delay receiving money from your RSP until you have to convert it over to a Registered Retirement Income Fund (RRIF). Or, you may want to start receiving a monthly payment right away if you are worried about the Old Age Security (OAS) claw back or if you don't have a work pension plan.

Estate planning is not the most enjoyable thing to discuss, as you are planning for your passing and your wishes for the transfer of your assets. But, the **transfer** stage discussion may be the most important part of the financial planning process, as this is when you can make sure your final wishes are followed through with and your legacy is carried out the way you want. Whether this includes passing your estate down to your children or including charitable donations, this is important to discuss with your legal professional and update when necessary. Right from the start of the financial planning process, you should make sure your will and power of attorney's are updated and reviewed on a regular basis, as your personal situation or government rules can change.

Sharper

- On a piece of paper make a list of everything that would potentially be lost if you were not able to work for 3 months and then 1 year. Also, if you were to never work again.

- If you and your spouse / partner have minor dependents, what would happen if you were to die in a common disaster and neither of you had a will?

- If you have a retirement plan in place how long will you be able to live without having to rely only on government benefits?

CHAPTER 16

More Than One Timeline

The best thing about the future is that it comes one day at a time. - **Abraham Lincoln**

Initiating
Conversations

Do you plan for today or do you plan for tomorrow?

Do you worry about outliving your retirement nest egg?

Do you have a plan in place to support your parent's in their elder years?

A timeline is a great illustration to show the different events that will happen in the future, even if they are just 'penciled' in. Your unique timeline can consist of goals in life that you would like to accomplish (graduate from university, buy a house, get married, retire) and the approximate monetary value that you need to experience it, if applicable. Your financial planner will sit down with you and research the information that is known (OAS, CPP, company pension plan) and create hypothetical illustrations on all other investments that don't have a guaranteed value at a certain date in the future (RSP, TFSA, non-registered).

I enjoy today, but want to plan for tomorrow, so I can enjoy it also.

Questions that your financial planner will need to ask you to fill out your financial planning timeline:

* When are you going to buy your home?

* When are you going to have children?

* When do you want to retire?

* How long do you expect to live?

Yes I do because you never know how long your retirement is going to last.

A great start to your timeline involves a simple exercise. All you need to do is take a piece of 8 ½ x 11 paper and turn it so that the long side is horizontal. Take a pencil and draw a horizontal line through the middle of the page. Write the current year over the left starting point of the line and the year to which you believe you will live to at the end point of the line. The length of the line will depend on how old you currently are and how many special dates you want to include on the timeline. For example, we will use a 25 year old married couple named Arnold and Elaine who have recently graduated from university and landed their first jobs. Their grandparents have lived well into their 90s, so they will be using age 90 as an end point. Arnold and Elaine input the following information:

- Age 28, they would like to have their first child.

- Age 30, they would like to buy their first home.

- Age 31, they would like to have their second child.

- Age 55, they would like to be mortgage free.

- Age 60, they would both like to be retired.

- Age 75, they will plan to lower their retirement income needs as most of their travelling would be done between ages 60 and 75. They also add in the appropriate years for OAS and CPP income.

Now that the important life events are included in your timeline, it is time to input different numbers that will define the amount of money that needs to be saved for the retirement years and a comfortable rate of return during retirement. First, determine the amount you want to have saved for your retirement years. Once this number is determined, you need to go to present day and figure out what amount of money and return expectations are needed to meet the retirement goal. This number may scare Arnold and Elaine in this example, but they need to start somewhere. Other information that will eventually need a dollar figure attached in the timeline is: how much they are able to save for a down payment, the amount of money they are able to invest, the projected costs of raising two children, pension statements, and so on.

It is important to update your timeline on a regular basis (i.e. during your yearly review) and when there is a life event that needs to be changed (retirement date) or isn't already included (loss of job). Updated statements from all investments, pensions, etc. are important, as this will show you if you are on the right track to meet the investments needed to fulfill all the goals that are listed on the timeline.

I do worry about not having enough money if my parents need assistance during their later years so I need to plan accordingly with my siblings.

If it works for you, you may want to include the ages of others who will be part of your financial planning timeline, such as your children and parents, as this will assist you further in planning for the future.

Living for today and not tomorrow will make future decisions even more difficult. The shortfall dollar figure that you will initially define may seem to be unattainable, but that is why you start as early as you can. If you don't, then it may be too late to alter your numbers when you realize that some of your life goals will not be met or experienced the way you would have wanted or felt you deserved. You want to be able to control the ability to accomplish your 'working years' standard of living and live a retirement lifestyle that you work hard to enjoy. Many people like to work hard and play hard, but you have to plan smart so that you can look back at the planning that you have done and smile to yourself knowing that it was a job well done.

Sharper Focus

- Set up a time in the next week to create your own financial timeline.

- Discuss your financial timeline the next time you meet with your financial planner.

- Crunch the numbers in your own financial timeline and create a couple of alternative timelines providing options in case you are not able to meet certain goals, the amount of investments decline or increase, or if your return expectations are not met.

CHAPTER 17

Rainy Day Funds

*Don't knock the weather. If it didn't change once in a while,
nine out of ten people couldn't start a conversation.*
- Kin Hubbard (1868-1930)

Initiating
Conversations

*What happens if you don't have an
emergency fund and need access to one
right away?*

*Do you use your credit card or line of credit
as your 'emergency fund'?*

*How much should you save for an
emergency fund?*

Two constants in my house: First, it is true that my wife or my in-laws couldn't start a conversation if the weather didn't change. I guess it comes from the family history of farming. Second, everyone knows who Wayne is—and now that he has retired from the local TV scene, we are looking for another meteorologist to spend part of the dinner hour with. To my son, Wayne was the only weatherman he knew for his first five years. My daughter could even recognize his name and wave to him at two years old. I wish I had the Hawaiian shirt wardrobe he has. I have always wanted to ask him if the correct 'weather lingo' is "the sun is coming out" or "the clouds are moving" as a ridge of high pressure hits right above my neighbourhood.

Change my budget and possibility my standard of living.

My only academic experience with the weather was taking an atmosphere course that qualified for my science credit at college. In the class I learned about low and high pressure systems, rain, and storms—among other important atmosphere information—that made me look smart at home in the months following finishing the course.

From a financial perspective, my interest in the weather is about wondering if everyone has a *rainy day fund*. In a financial planning

textbook, this fund would be defined as an *emergency fund*. Whatever it is called, it is important to save for those unexpected events in your life that cause you to spend money from a reactive perspective rather than a proactive basis.

The amount of money to save in your rainy day fund can vary, but a good place to start is three to five months of net income. The further you are away from meeting this goal the more that your variable expenses would need to be adjusted if you don't have any money designated for your rainy day fund. For most people, extra money goes to an increase in lifestyle expenses or to pay off debt.

A good discipline to have is to build your rainy day fund by adding it as a fixed expense in your monthly budget. During low interest rate environments, it may be tempting to rely on a line of credit (LOC) for your rainy day

Line of credit.

fund. It may work for some, but if you are unable to pay down your LOC balance with future positive cash flow, then it is not a good solution. Having access to a LOC at the start is of value, but hopefully you will never have to use it as your rainy day fund.

Having to use your rainy day fund can be due to inconveniences such as your furnace breaking down or your car needing repairs. You can use the fund to pay up front for the replacement costs and then start to build it up again (as monthly contributions continue to be a fixed expense) with future savings as your regular cash flow and budget won't be changing.

Another need for your rainy day fund could be to support yourself during a loss of income for a period of time due to job layoff or injury.

Just because the income disappears for a period of time doesn't mean that the monthly costs will cease. This is a danger of not setting up a rainy day fund or not having access to a LOC. Without an income for a longer period of time you may not have luck in asking the bank for a LOC unless you have equity built up in your house. Once any group benefits and other personal benefit coverages you have are used up, you will need access to other assets for as long as possible until deeper changes would have to be made in your overall budget.

Three to five months net income.

Having a rainy day fund will delay the need to withdraw money from your registered plans and other investments. If you are relying on your investments as your rainy day fund you may not be able to choose when to withdraw your investment funds. You may be in a situation where a withdrawal is needed when it would have a negative effect from a tax perspective or the stock market is experiencing a bad case of volatility.

Your rainy day fund should consist of term deposits, cashable GICs and other types of investments that have minimal market volatility. Some people prefer to lump their rainy day fund holdings into equities because they don't want to lose any potential growth in an investment that they will 'never need' which is one of those 'it will never happen to me' beliefs. But to others risk in any format in a rainy day fund is not part of the conversation.

To illustrate using a few borrowed terms from Wayne, you need to have a rainy day fund for the life moments when low pressure systems bring dark clouds and storms. But at the same time don't be overly optimistic that life is always full of high pressure systems where the sun shines bright and you will never need to use a rainy day fund.

Sharper Focus

- Make an effort to ask your friends if they have a rainy day fund and how hard it is to save for it.

- Ask your parent's what they used to cover any emergencies during the early years of their marriage or even today.

- Set a goal to invest a percentage of your monthly income into a rainy day account that is specifically only for a rainy day and not used for whenever you need extra money

CHAPTER 18

What is My Credit Score?

Remember that credit is money. – **Benjamin Franklin**

Initiating Conversations

When did you receive your first credit card and what was the limit?

When you received your first credit card did you understand all the 'legalese'?

Do you believe in having credit?

One day after picking my son up from school we visited a local McDonald's ® drive thru for a treat. As we approached the pay window I pulled out my credit card to pay and asked my son if he knew what the blue card was for. It was a 'teachable' moment as I tried to explain to my 5 year old that my blue credit card 'is money'. I explained to him that I will receive a bill in the mail in the future with the total to pay. If I don't pay the bill then I will pay a penalty and may not be able to use my credit card in the future.

$500 during my first year of college.

It's not like when I was growing up where cash was mainly used. These days I am sure children will rarely see their parent's use cash as we are in a 'less cash' society. As Canada has turned one- and two- dollar bills into coins and stopped producing pennies what will it stop producing next? Will the future ever be a 'credit and debit only' society?

Credit cards seem to be easy to get, but you have to be careful when you use credit. You can just as easy have credit ruin the life you want to build. Using credit in the wrong way will create headaches for you in the future when you really could use more credit.

I have to admit that I have done something like this more than once. I have walked down the hallway at a Canucks game to see that a credit

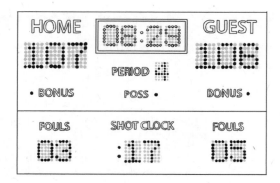

card company is giving out free blankets that would fit my son's bed quite well. But there is a catch: I have to fill out an application for a credit card. I don't need the credit, but what can it hurt?

I remember my first credit card application. I was in the first month of classes at my local college and I wanted to subscribe to several magazines with some of the money I was making at my part-time job. It must have been important to the credit card company because I was going to receive the student discount. Since I was a student with not much earned income I must have been a great credit risk as I was offered a credit card for $500 by basically just signing my name. I still remember the day as I stood in my parent's living room opening my mail and finding my credit card. I just wanted to go out on a $500 shopping spree! I am glad I was wise at that time and knew it was not my money to spend if I couldn't afford to pay the balance owing each month.

No. Didn't understand much! I wish I had someone explain it to me!

Depending on what you read, who you listen to, or watch on television, you will get different views on how much credit is good and whether you should have credit at all. What does a credit lender look at before you are approved?

Your credit score: Whether you apply to a major credit card company or your local department store, the lender is looking at the risk that they will be taking on if they approve a credit limit to you. The lender is looking at how you have done with credit in the past and therefore predicts the risk you will be in the future.

Credit reporting agencies in Canada have different credit scores, but in general the lender is looking for a higher score. They may even use the credit score to determine the amount of your credit limit and interest rate charged depending on your credit history with other lenders. The same information will be taken if you are applying for additional credit with the same or different lender.[1]

Defining your credit rating: Different credit ratings are referenced in the resource section of www.financialfotographs.com. In general, your credit rating on each type of credit you have will often have a letter and number attached to your score. You can find numbers one to nine with one being that you pay all your bills on time and nine being that you are bankrupt, have bad debt or in collections. The letters I, O or R (should be I. O. U.) define the credit that you are using depending on whether the debt is credit by installments (car loan), open credit (line of credit), or revolving credit (credit cards).[2]

Establishing credit: In order to establish a credit score you need to establish short-term debt. To do this, you may want to pay for your groceries, phone bill, or other small expenses by the use of your credit card. As soon as you get home, log on to your bank and transfer the amount of your bill from your banking account directly to your credit card. This way you are just briefly borrowing money, but in the end establishing a history of paying off your debt on time.

Pay your bills on time: When I receive my credit card statement in the mail I always go online and pay the minimum required and then set a reminder in my calendar to pay my balance in full two business days prior to the deadline. It is very important that you pay your minimum right away just in case you miss your balance due date for a couple days or even until you get a reminder in the mail the next month when your next statement is received. Everyone will likely miss a deadline or

[1,2] Equifax Canada / Industry Canada Website
[2]

two in their lifetime and if your minimum is not at least paid before the deadline you could run into extra problems with your credit card issuer.

Having more than one credit card: Some people like having a couple of credit cards from major suppliers depending on what the retailer accepts or the type of benefits you receive from using different cards.

Receiving gifts and gadgets when you apply for credit cards might be fun but it can hurt your credit score the more you have your credit checked when applying for those additional credit cards. Also, if you apply for additional credit in the future and you have multiple active credit cards (even if you have activated them but never used them) the new credit card company may offer you additional credit but will only consider this after your total existing available limit is taken into consideration (as if you have maxed out all available credit).

Yes, only if you can control its use.

People often don't realize when applying for a home mortgage that your credit rating is pulled by each lender that you approach to lend you money. This could hurt your credit score but lenders should understand the circumstance you are in. An alternative is if you use a mortgage broker your credit will be pulled once and used for the number of lenders your mortgage broker uses.

Increase your credit rating: Pay your bills on time and always pay the balance in full. Using your credit card for all of your spending is good when used for tracking purposes, but make sure that you are keeping within your budget. If it gets too difficult, you will need to use your debit card for some purchases. However, using your debit card is not helping build your credit rating. If you are concerned about overspending, put a limit on your credit card that you know you can pay each month.

Getting a co-signer for my credit: This may get you the credit you need (depending on the co-signers credit rating) but the liability is jointly held and you will not be building up your credit rating as fast. It is a last effort if nothing else is working.

Pay nothing for 12 months or more: It may be tempting to make a purchase with no payments or interest for 12 months. This can be dangerous if you don't pay in full by the due date. There will likely be interest and penalties attached. Make sure you read the fine print. If you are smart with your money you could accept the deal from the retailer but put the money you would have used for the purchase in a savings account to be withdrawn one month or so before the due date to pay the bill outstanding. You could make a few extra dollars but the temptation to use this money may be too much for you to handle. If this is the case you should pay today and enjoy your purchase knowing that it has been paid in full.

Credit and lines of credit: A line of credit is often provided at a lower interest rate compared to a normal credit card. This could be used for a portion of a mortgage balance, consolidating other debt or just to have for future needs. A line of credit is often based on the assets that you have on top of your credit rating and score.

Credit balance transfers to lower paying credit cards: In a competitive marketplace among credit card lenders you will find deals that will enable you to transfer your credit card balance to another credit card company for a period of time and at a lower rate. This can seem like a great deal but this often means that you are in trouble with your monthly budget and spending habits as you are not able to re-pay your credit card balance in full each month. Lower credit interest rates are often tempting but make sure you understand the balance transfer fee, the length of the low rate, and what the rate will be if you don't pay the balance in full prior to the rate going back to the normal lending rate.

Sharper Focus

- Ask your friends about what their credit card experiences have been like.

- Ask your parent's when they applied for their first credit card and how they managed the temptation of spending on credit. Did they always pay their balances each month?

- If you know that you have been having trouble with your credit history, ask your financial planner how you could create better credit habits.

CHAPTER 19

What do My Groceries Cost?

I don't mind going back to daylight savings time. With inflation, the hour will be the only thing I've saved all year.
– Victor Borge

Initiating Conversations

Do you include inflation in your financial plan?

If you had a conversation with your parents or grandparents about the effects of inflation, what do you think they might say?

How do you think inflation will affect your financial situation in the next 5 or 10 years?

On most sunny days in the morning, if the sun shines at a perfect angle through the upstairs window to our living room, you can see the dust in the air. Try explaining this to a two year old who thinks it is 'fluff' and doesn't like 'fluff' anywhere in the house.

Yes, it is very important.

This is a perfect example of inflation; something you can't see but need to deal with when you are a consumer or an investor. Inflation eats away at your purchasing power and it should be included into financial planning discussions with your financial planner. The future is uncertain and being pro-active rather than re-active is important when developing your financial plan whether you are planning for the next 5, 10 years, or more.

My grandma gave me back a postcard I was going to mail to her in the late 1970s or early 80s that included a stamp showing me how much the price of a stamp for a regular piece of mail was back then. Now, Canada Post sells us a 'P' stamp where the cost of mailing a regular letter will not be more than the stamp. Therefore, if you think inflation is going up then it may be wise to buy more 'P' stamps than you need today than wait to buy them in the future. Personally, I would have called it the 'NIP stamp' for 'No Increases I Promise'.

The Consumer Price Index (CPI) is the common meas- *Always act as* ure of inflation. It measures the changes in the aver- *though inflation* age price of a basket of goods purchased in Canada *is going to be* within a specific time frame. The 'basket' is made up *higher than it is.* of food, shelter, household operations, furnishings and equipment, clothing and footwear, transportation, health and personal care, education, recreation, and reading, alcoholic beverages and tobacco products[1]. Each piece of the 'basket' has a different weight, depending on the frequency of purchase. For instance, the price volatility of food is more important than purchases of clothing and footwear when calculating CPI. The 'core CPI' to measure the trend of inflation excludes fruit, vegetables, gasoline, fuel oil, natural gas, mortgage interest, intercity transportations, and tobacco products, as they are classified as the most volatile[2].

Effects of high inflation can create a sense of worry because people will be unsure of how the future will look for them. Current decisions are easier than longer term goals in this environment as inflation is often unpredictable. GIC rates can become worthy of investing as rates will be higher, but you have to take away the inflation rate and taxes to get a realistic rate of return. Remember that returns can be big, but the most important thing is what you have in your pocket after selling a particular investment. You may want to cut down on your spending during this time period so that you have a cushion. With costs going up, you can make sure that you have enough money for your fixed costs and prioritize your variable costs when looking at your monthly budget. A high rate of inflation is tough on people who receive a pension or a salary that does not increase by the rate of inflation. Cost of living goes up due to inflation, but the income coming into the home is not keeping pace.

---

[1] www.statcan.gc.ca – Date Modified: 2013-3-21

[2] Bank of Canada – www.bankofcanada.ca

Effects of low inflation can create a sense of calm because people can manage current budgets and long term planning more easily. People tend to look more favourably on borrowing money to invest or to buy a home as rates are more favourable. The question then is the term of the loan, which will be dependent on your feelings on the long term outlook of inflation. A low rate of inflation is much easier on those who receive a pension or monthly salary that is not tied to the rate of inflation, as there won't be much impact on their monthly cash flow as there is if inflation is high.[3]

Listed below are other common words you will hear as the economy changes.

Deflation – a consecutive fall of the CPI created negative inflation being recorded during the Great Depression of the 1930s as inflation fell by more than 20 percent. An example that is not classified as deflation is when you see a decrease in prices of electronics due to technological advances. However, consistent deflation over a period of time can add uncertainty to the decisions that the government makes, and therefore possible negative effects on economic growth.

I will need to save more.

Disinflation – a CPI increase that slowly decreases over a period of time. For example, Year 1 the CPI could be at 7%, Year 2 the increase could be 6%, and then Year 3 the increase could be 2%.

---

[3] Bank of Canada – www.bankofcanada.ca

Stagflation – a combination of 'stagnation'—slow economic growth and relatively high unemployment, combined with inflation. For example, stagflation occurred in the 1970s when oil prices increased without economic growth following suit.

Hyperinflation – this occurs when inflation is completely out of control. For example, if a country experiences a depression, the government might put a large inflow of currency into the economy with no matching economic growth. When this happens there is no balance between the economic definition of supply and demand and the country's currency loses value due to the increase in prices of goods everywhere.[4]

Each time you go to the grocery store you may have a different list to follow. It's a good idea to keep track of your grocery costs on a monthly basis to give you a better idea when certain items are actually on sale rather than at the regular or an increased price. An official 'sale' and 'reduced to sell' are too different definitions of a sale. You also have to realize when a sale is not actually a sale because you never see what the price of the same item was last time you shopped at that same store.

You also want to make sure you stick to your grocery list as much as possible as we all know that the word 'sale' affects people's will-power differently. Straying from your list can create your own 'inflation' of your grocery bill not because the actual cost of your grocery items went up but because you bought items that in the end were not needed but bought anyway.

---

[4]   investopedia.com

Sharper Focus

- Start to collect your grocery bill each time you shop to become familiar with what the regular prices of items are so that you are better educated with your spending habits.

- Ask your parent's and grandparent's how they reacted to different inflation rates in their lifetime and how they may have changed their habits to be better prepared the next time.

- Ask your financial planner how you can prepare your budgeting habits and financial plan to be ready for an increase or decrease of inflation in your lifetime.

CHAPTER 20

Revisiting Risk

There are risks and costs to a program of action. But they are far less than the long-range risks and costs of comfortable inaction. – **John F. Kennedy**

Initiating
Conversations

Do you think your risk level for investments should be lower during retirement than in your working years?

Do you know what your investment risk level is?

Is it important to revisit risk when you get married?

Risk can mean different things to different people at different stages in life. Knowing what risk means to you is very important as it affects the decisions that you make now and in the future when following your financial plan. Below is a list of different risks associated with investing and your financial plan. These are important to know so that you can develop your own interpretation of each type of risk and understand how to build it into your financial plan.

Protection

Health benefits during retirement – It is very important to check well before retirement if your group benefits will carry over for your total retirement years, a portion of your retirement, or not at all. Things can change in the future, but having a health cost put into your overall retirement plan will help pay for expenses that are not covered in retirement or are not covered at the rate provided during your working years.

Life insurance – If you don`t have enough money to meet your investment asset goals upon your passing, you don't want to run the risk of dying prior to your goals being met. Therefore, it is wise to consider life insurance coverage that will take the place of not meeting your asset targets. You should continue this approach until you have met your goals or the life insurance is too expensive for your budget and then you will have to re-think your asset goals.

Disability – You don't want to run the risk of not being able to maintain your standard of living for a period of time. If your employee benefits don't meet your standard of living goals, then it would be wise to consider a personal disability plan. The plan will

> *Yes, losses during retirement will be tougher to make up.*

most likely be more expensive than your group benefit plan, as the risk to the insurance company is only you and not spread over many employees.

Critical illness – The chance of morbidity (coming down with an illness) is more likely than mortality (dying) the longer we live. Therefore, it is important to consider this risk by seeing if critical illness coverage is right for you. Again, it comes down to your budget and health, but having a sum of money come to you if you do experience a critical illness and survive is a good plan to have, as it would help you from having to rush back to work when you are not 100% ready.

Accumulation

Investing – Before you invest any of your assets, you should complete a risk tolerance questionnaire with your financial planner. The questionnaire and the questions your planner will ask you will either validate what you believe your risk tolerance is or create a need for further discussion. In the end, the money is yours to invest as you'd like, but due diligence is your financial planner`s role.

Inflation – Planning for inflation is an important part of your financial plan. Even though you can look to past inflation rates, you have to plan for a reasonable amount of inflation going forward. Your investment projections should be adjusted each year to set realistic future inflation goals. The planned standard of living you project to use in the future to meet your goals should be adjusted for taxes and inflation. Not including these deductions will make you feel like you have more money than you actually do. Look for 'in your pocket income' and not 'on paper' income.

Currency – If you are investing in a Canadian mutual fund that has investments outside of Canada, the changes in the Canadian dollar compared to other global currencies could have an effect on your over-all investment return. For an extra management cost, some funds utilize 'hedging' to limit this currency risk.

No, I should complete a risk tolerance questionnaire with my planner.

Interest rates – If you are invested in fixed income investments (bonds), a rise or fall of interest rates will affect their price and the returns.

Political –Before putting your investment dollars into another country's market, you should consider its political landscape, tax structure, inflation control, laws, and other economic policies.

Sector – Having too much of your money invested in a particular sector (i.e. financial companies, gold) could create extra volatility in your investment portfolio.

Liquidity – There are all kinds of investments to consider in the marketplace. One of the first questions you should ask is how liquid are your holdings within your portfolio. If you know of a redemption need in the future, you want to make sure that you know the waiting period of each of your investments. Is the pricing of your investment done on a daily, weekly, or monthly basis? How much time in advance do you need to give to request a redemption in your account?

Conversion

Pension – If your pension does not increase by the standard of living, you have the risk of not keeping up with your standard of living costs. Therefore, you will need to adjust your budget accordingly.

Government benefits – With an ever changing economy, you won`t know exactly what your government benefits (i.e. OAS and CPP) will look like once you decide to retire. When projecting your retirement income, you can include the government benefits at current rates and at projected rates so that you can plan for additional investments accordingly. As more and more baby boomers retire, there will be fewer people contributing to the future funding of retirement benefits. As a result the government will receive less tax revenue (unless they raise taxes) and it is likely for those of us working now to have lower government benefits in retirement. Therefore, it is wise to not rely 100% on being able to maintain your desired retirement standard of living on government benefits but to supplement your retirement with personal savings.

Retirement – the risk of outliving your money in retirement becomes more likely the longer you live. Therefore, you may want to make sure this doesn't happen by: working part time for some of your retirement, creating an 'active' phase of your retirement (travelling and being as active as your health allows), and creating a 'local' phase of retirement (when your health and costs don't allow you to go far). This will assist you as you create realistic spending plans for both the 'active' phase and the 'local' phase. Your estate plan needs to be an important part also so

> *Yes.*
> *It is important to create a combined risk tolerance as needed rather than keeping everything separate.*

that your retirement needs (money) doesn't affect your legacy plans. If too much money is spent then you will need to change your legacy plans or start to draw from assets that you wanted to leave to your heirs.

The sooner you plan the better, as if you wait until you actually retire, you will most likely not be able to enjoy the retirement the way you deserve.

Taxes – The risk of having no tax plan will affect your net 'in your pocket' amount of retirement income. You should plan on how to utilize all income sources (RSP, spousal RSP, TFSA, pension, OAS, CPP, non-registered) in the most beneficial way. It is nice to receive a tax break when you contribute to your RRSP, but you also want the future tax bill to be at a lower tax bracket than when you initially contributed. That's why it's important to use realistic projections when using personal investments (RSP, spousal RSP, TFSA, and pension) and for government benefits (CPP, OAS).

Bucket list – Time and money are two ways to create a living legacy for you. If you don't plan ahead while you are healthy, then you may run the risk of not doing everything you set out to do in your life. The best way to create a plan is to write down everything you would like to do and discuss with your financial planner. Together you can create a realistic list and prioritize in order of importance compared to your retirement budget. If the money is not going to be there, then you may want to re-work your budget to see if any money can be found by re-prioritizing other spending habits. Starting your bucket list should be done in your earning years so that the costs associated can be planned for early on.

Transfer

Your will – Not having a will creates problems carrying out your final wishes. Do you want the government to make decisions for you? If not, it is important to have a will and keep it updated.

Power of Attorney – With the likelihood of illness coming before death, it is important that you elect someone of your choosing to take care of all your financial, property, and health decisions if you are unable to make sound decisions.

Estate Planning– If you can do an estate tax projection, you can re-work your financial plan accordingly. You may decide you don't want to leave money to your beneficiaries at death, but instead would like to gift it while you are living. (You have to be careful that this won't create financial hardship later on in your life.) You may also wish to have an insurance plan in place to cover your estate taxes. This should be discussed with your financial planner sooner rather than later, as the cost goes up with age and is dependent on your health at application.

Sharper Focus

- Make a list of what you would like to accomplish in your lifetime and what risks could prevent you from meeting each goal.

- Without asking your parent's or grandparent's what their net worth is ask them if they increased or decreased their tolerance to risk as they got older or during retirement.

- Ask your friends if they are meeting their financial planning objectives and how they have changed their definition of risk over the past 5-10 years.

CHAPTER 21

Recession, Recovery and the Alphabet

The economy is showing encouraging signs of recovery.

- **George Voinovich**

Initiating
Conversations

How can you build a financial plan that will react well to stock market volatility?

Do you look at a market recovery as an investment opportunity or further risk?

What can you do if you hear the term 'it is different this time' when it comes to commentary on the markets?

There are two questions that I am asked on a regular basis when it comes to stock market volatility. If the market is doing well: "How high can the market go?" If the market is doing poorly: "When will the market recover?" Either way, an investor wants to know whether to buy or sell depending on the current market cycle.

If the market always went up, the only thing that you would know for sure is that as long as you stay in the market, you will make more money than the investors who entered after you. This would be the ultimate 'Buy and Hold' strategy but also the 'too good to be true' scenario at the same time. The market is always volatile, but everyone has a different definition and comfort level for each level of volatility the market goes through each year. If you are a stock picker, then price and growth of stocks is your main concern. From a financial planning perspective, price, growth and planned date of withdrawal(s) are concerns.

Try to be as pro-active as possible to limit the times you need to be re-active.

To illustrate how volatility affects an investment portfolio, I use the example of taking a yo-yo up a flight of stairs. The first step is where you are today. The last step at the top is where you hope to be in the future to meet a particular financial planning goal. The yo-yo is the volatility of the stock market. The steps upward are the hopeful values of your investment portfolio at different points of time in the future. The best scenario would be to get from point A to point B without any volatility (i.e., no movement of the yo-yo), but that is not realistic. The only way to limit the volatility of the market would be to invest in GIC type investments. This is where your principle is guaranteed but growth potential is limited to the interest rate you receive and the distance from point A to point B may be longer than you would like.

The price, and therefore the volatility, of a particular investment is often reflective of how the current market is doing. All markets around the world experience recessions and recoveries at different times of the year and for different lengths of time. So your investment portfolio should have a pro-active approach rather than a re-active approach as much as possible. To make matters worse, it is often not easy to recognize a recession or recovery until further economic research is completed and the histories of similar markets are examined.

Economists often look at *'leading'* and *'lagging'* indicators when trying to predict an economic cycle. Since stocks are priced depending on a shareholder's future expectation, the stock market is seen as a leading indicator. A lagging indicator would be employment, as business owners wait until they feel confident that the market will recover before they decide to hire additional employees to meet a growing need for products.[1]

Visualizing different letters from the alphabet can help an investor understand markets that are in recession or moving to recovery.

L-Shaped Market Recession/Recovery –With an L-shaped market the economy would see a drastic drop as this economic downturn has 'doomsday' written all over it.[2] The 'flat-line' would not be the death of the market, but just a long time of waiting until the market's 'heartbeat'

---

[1] http://www.moneycrashers.com/leading-lagging-economic-indicators/

[2] http://www.davemanuel.com/investor-dictionary/l-shaped-depression/

got stronger. An example of this type of recession/ recovery would be Japan in the 1990s. During this time Japan experienced a multi-year depression due to the bubble bursting in real estate prices and the stock market.[3]

It all depends on what my financial planning needs are at the time.

U-Shaped Market Recession/Recovery – This is a slower economic version of a V-shaped recovery. The economy will take longer to recover and investors will need to be patient for the recovery to happen. An example of this type of recession would be what happened in the US between 1971 and 1978.[4]

V-Shaped Market Recession/Recovery – The market will recover as fast as it fell, which is a breath of fresh air in a volatile market. Examples of a V-Shaped recovery would be in the US between 1990 and 1991 and during 2001. Out of the four 'letter recoveries' the V-shape would be first on an investor's wish list.[5]

W-Shaped Market Recession/Recovery – The market will show signs of recovery for a short period of time but then take another dip downward before a stronger recovery presents itself. Investors need to be careful that they don't react too quickly to a false-start recovery. A W-shaped recession/recovery is also known as a 'double-dip recession'.

An example would be the 1980 US recession that had a double dip in 1981 and 1982.[6]

If you are able to predict correctly how a market would react to an economic recession and recovery, you would be a very popular person. But one of the aspects of making money in the market is to make sure that your investments meet your risk tolerance and timeline. This way

---

[3] http://www.davemanuel.com/investor-dictionary/l-shaped-depression/

[4] http://www.learningmarkets.com/understanding-v-u-w-and-l-shaped-recessions/.

[5] http://www.learningmarkets.com/understanding-v-u-w-and-l-shaped-recessions/

[6] http://www.learningmarkets.com/understanding-v-u-w-and-l-shaped-recessions/

Seek out family and friends who have experienced market volatility in the past and ask them how they reacted.

the money will be available to you with the least amount of volatility. If you look at a specific economy over a reasonable period of time, you will see one or more of the above market recession and recovery letters of the alphabet. By working with a financial planner, you can put an investment plan in place that will be able to help you weather any market storm.

Sharper Focus

- During your next review meeting ask your financial planner to explain to you what type of market volatility the economy is experiencing.

- Ask a friend or family member that has been investing longer than you how they have reacted to different market cycles in the past and what lessons they have learned.

- Ask your financial planner how your plan is situated to be as proactive as possible to any future volatility so that you can still meet your financial planning goals.

CHAPTER 22

The Taxing Rollercoaster

*I'm involved in the stock market, which is fun and,
sometimes, very painful.* – **Regis Philbin**

Initiating
Conversations

*Do you like to let your investments 'ride' or
do you like to review them on a regular basis?*

*How much emphasis would you put on past
growth when compared to future potential
growth of your investments?*

*Is it important to review the returns of
investments before or after taxes?*

Have you heard someone say "the stock market is like a rollercoaster?"
When I was younger, I took a few rides on the Wooden Roller Coaster
in Vancouver, BC. While on the ride I thought to myself "why did I do
this?" and then got right back on again.

Depending on the market cycle your portfolio is going
through, it may seem like a rollercoaster with it's up and
down momentum with very few 'flat lines'. I am sure that

*Review on
a regular
basis.*

you would prefer to ride the big rollercoaster, but have your investment portfolio simulate the 'kiddie coaster ride'. At least the drop at
the Vancouver ride is not as much as the 81 degree drop riding the
'Outlaw Run' in Branson, Missouri USA (I have not done this yet) but
in times of fear and volatility in the stock market you like the climb up
and you don't like the drop down. Risk is a big part in any investment
choice that you make and, as history has taught us, we have to be able
to understand the risk that we are taking so that the portfolio that we
choose can handle whichever rollercoaster the market decides to ride
during your individual investment timeframe. At least with the market
you can get out whenever you like (most times), unlike the one chance
with a rollercoaster—at the end.

Most investments that you make are tied to a particular financial planning goal that you have. Whether it is a down payment for your first home, education for your children, or retirement funds, each goal has a particular timeline for which you will need the money. With each unique timeline comes a specific risk tolerance that you can handle.

Good to look at past performance, but look to the future outlook, as there is no promise of history repeating itself.

Here is a list of a few investment terms that you should know to assist in your investment strategy. Hopefully it will help you avoid the roller-coaster rides of the market (more detailed examples of each term will be available on the resource section at www.financialfotographs.com):

Compound interest (advantages of early investing) – If you invest a Loonie and you earn a 10% return during the first year, your investment would be worth $1.10. If you re-invested the $1.10 and you earn another 10% return in the following year, your investment would be worth $1.21 at the end of the year. This is an example of compound interest. Money is making money on itself by re-investing all gains. The earlier you start the better as time is on your side.

Rule of 72 – With this rule you are trying to figure out how long it will take to double your money by dividing 72 by the growth rate (%). For example, if the growth rate is 1% per year, your money will double in 72 years. If you make 6% per year, your money will double in 12 years. If you make 9% per year, your money will double in 8 years.

Diversification – This rule is to assist in spreading out the risk of your total investment portfolio over a number of investments, whether it is with a number of different stocks, a number of different bonds, or even a number of GICs with different maturity dates. You are trying to get to the same goal, but you want to diversify the risk in case a few investments don't get the return you want.

Dollar cost averaging – This is the rule where you may like to have a bit of extra volatility when you invest a certain amount of money on a regular basis. For example, you invest $100 on the 15th of each month. Depending on the price of your investment, you could be buying it on a down or up day and receiving the appropriate shares. This can work against you if you are withdrawing money on a regular basis, especially if the market is on a downward trend.

Now let's talk about tax!

Returning to our rollercoaster, once you get off, it's time to pay for your next ride (unless you have an unlimited day pass which would not work for this illustration!). On the investment rollercoaster it is the tax you are subject to depending on the type of gain or distribution you are receiving (capital gains, dividends or interest) and what type of program it is invested in (non-registered, RRSP, RRIF, TFSA etc.). Tax rates are listed in the resource section at www.financialfotographs. com.

Non-registered Investments

Interest – if you have a GIC or bond that is giving you interest income, then the total income is taxed at your marginal tax rate.

Dividend – If your investment is giving you dividend income, then the income will be 'grossed up' at the appropriate rate, a dividend tax credit is applied, and then you are taxed at your marginal tax rate.

Capital gains – If you have a capital gain upon selling your investment the gross gain gets deducted at the appropriate rate and then the net amount is taxed at your marginal tax rate.

Return of capital - If you invest in a product with a return of capital feature and start receiving withdrawals you have to be careful to keep extra good notes on the money that you withdraw. The reason for this is that each withdrawal will include a portion of your own money which will not be taxable. Once all your original investment is returned to you and there is a remaining balance all withdrawals from that point forward will be fully taxable.

After taxes, as this is what you will be working with in the end.

Registered Investments (RRSP, RRIF, TFSA)

Any investment within your portfolio that is invested in one or all of these registered accounts will still receive the same interest, dividend, capital gain, or return of capital distributions as you would in a non-registered account, but the corresponding tax implications are not the same. This is because the government only cares about the end number that you withdrawal out of your registered plan. This withdrawal will not be subject to interest, dividend, or capital gains tax. The withdrawal will be treated similar to any earned income you have in that it is taxed at your marginal tax rate without any tax credits (e.g. capital gain or dividend tax credit). You would have received a tax deduction upon investing into your RSP in the past. As for TFSA withdrawals, there is no tax applicable regardless of the amount of gain earned. The reason here is that you originally invested in your TFSA with after tax dollars.

A question you should ask your financial planner is if it would make sense to build a registered portfolio with your equities in your TFSA and your fixed income, and GIC investments inside your RSP. Separate plans working together for the common goal of appropriate growth projections while limiting tax payable on growth as much as possible is a great mix.

With any investment, it is always wise to look at the potential tax situation in the future, as this may influence your initial investment. In most cases it is not your gross return that you are looking for, but your net (in your pocket) return. Investing with taxes in mind will assist you in controlling the future tax bill as much as possible (subject to the government changing the tax code).

As an investor you will always experience the peaks and valleys of the market. Outside of finding your comfort level with risk, you need to have regular reviews with your financial planner so that there are no tax surprises. By updating your financial plan on a regular basis and reviewing your investment portfolios and future tax liabilities appropriate changes can be made along the way.

Sharper Focus

- Ask your parents how they limited the amount of tax payable through regular reviews with their financial planner.

- Ask a friend how they manage their future tax liabilities with the different types of investments they make.

- Ask your grandparent's or parent's (if they are retired) what they wish they would have done differently if they believe they are currently paying too much tax.

CHAPTER 23

Diversification, Asset Allocation and a Piece of Pie

Career diversification ain't a bad thing. - **Vin Diesel**

Initiating Conversations

What is your definition of diversification?

Do you like to hit the 'homerun' with your investments but fear 'strikeouts'?

Do you feel like you have to keep certain investments because you like dealing with something familiar rather than something new?

I have used the illustration of a lemon meringue pie in the past when explaining the economic landscape that different countries have if the whole world was a pie. How big of a piece does Canada have? How big of a piece does the USA or Japan have? A simple but important example used to initiate a conversation with a client about diversification and asset allocation when it comes to their investment portfolio.

Diversification

Diversification can mean different things to different people. Some believe that diversification is having investments in a number of banks or a few investment portfolios with different investment advisors. Others believe that diversification is spreading your investment assets across many

The spreading out of my investment risk within a portfolio that meets my return expectations.

stocks or bonds. You can have diversification through pooled funds like mutual funds that combine your money along with other investors of the same fund and hold smaller portions of a number of equities and fixed income assets.

In the end diversification is an attempt to take an investor's money, invest the assets in a number of equities and fixed income holdings that will create opportunity for growth but limit the risk potential to the investor's risk tolerance. An important task to complete with any diversified portfolio is finding out the portfolio's 'correlation'. Correlation is the term given to the return relationships of each holding in a portfolio over a similar period of time. The longer time frame the better as time in the market gives you a better correlation picture. In a perfect world a diversified portfolio will have investments that are not 100% correlated together when compared to each other. Therefore, comparing two bank stocks

together should have a higher correlation than comparing a bank stock with a gold stock. Also, comparing an equity to a bond should have a low to negative correlation.

When discussing risk within a diversified portfolio you will have both systematic risk that can be defined as market risk and unsystematic risk which can be defined as business and financial risk.

Yes, but I need to find good investments and stay within my risk tolerance.

'*Investopedia*' explains systematic risk in the following manner: "interest rates, recession and political uncertainty all represent sources of systematic risk because they affect the entire market and cannot be avoided through diversification".[1] The only alternative is not to invest. Unsystematic risk is a risk that diversification will help you get rid of. The reason that this is possible is that the risk is associated to a particular investment[2]. Therefore, with additional research you can reduce the risk of your portfolio by spreading your money over a number of investments in a particular industry or over a number of industries.

Over diversification is a possibility and can be overcome as much as possible by proper investment research into individual investments but also different companies, countries and industries not only domestic

---

1 http://www.investopedia.com/terms/s/systematicrisk.asp
2 http://www.investopedia.com/terms/u/unsystematicrisk.asp

but around the world. Information is much easier to find with today's technology so it is important to use it. Risk vs. Reward is the ultimate goal within a diversified portfolio that will meet each investor's unique goals and objectives given a particular timeframe and risk tolerance.

Asset Allocation

I believe that asset allocation is the most important decision to make within an investor's investment portfolio as this takes into consideration their risk tolerance, future tax implications, investment horizon and the particular return projection the investor is anticipating. It is something that is not left alone but analyzed on a regular basis as personal or economic changes do occur during an investor's life time. Matching a potential asset allocation model to two different clients is not realistic and therefore an allocation should take into consideration as many important market and personal details as possible. Once the asset allocation of a portfolio is established and agreed upon the advisor can re-balance the portfolio as needed using the following techniques:

Strategic Asset Allocation – while taking into consideration the client's investment objective(s) and the market expectations a portfolio is created where the return expectation is maximized for a particular risk tolerance or minimized for a particular return expectation[3].

Dynamic Asset Allocation - an asset allocation is chosen at the beginning given an investor's risk tolerance and investment horizon. With an agreed upon percentage deviation (e.g. +/- 2%) or a particular timeframe (monthly or quarterly) the allocations are re-balanced back to the original allocation as long as the risk tolerance and investment horizon stay the same or another variable doesn't occur that creates a need to re-establish the chosen asset allocation sooner. An example would be if the dynamic asset allocation was 50% equities and 50% bonds and due to market movements the allocation became 60%

If a change would be better for my investment portfolio I would be open to discuss my options.

---

[3] CSI Global Education Inc. (2004) Chapter 5 page 5-11.

equities and 40% bonds at the end of a quarter then a re-balance back to 50% equities and 50% bonds would occur[4].

Tactical Asset Allocation – a strategic asset allocation process that can be deviated from for short periods of time due to the mangers future projections of equities or bonds and the holdings within those different asset classes. If the manager believes that equities will outperform bonds over the following three months, he or she may re-allocate more of the assets into equities for that timeframe, while at the same time always reviewing the portfolio to make sure no other additional changes need to be done in case the forecast was incorrect. Tools that the manager could use during these tactical calls are the movement of short-term interest rates, future inflation projections and specific growth rates in certain economic sectors[5].

So the next time you have a piece of pie, think about contacting your financial planner to make sure that your portfolio continues to meet the diversification and asset allocation model that you agreed to upon commencing your investment. At the same time ask your advisor if you should be discussing any changes in the next three months due to a life event or the future outlook of the market.

Sharper Focus

- Ask your parent's what portfolio diversification means to them.

- Contact your financial planner to review your current asset allocation.

- Ask your grandparent's if their portfolio asset allocation changed throughout the years.

---

4   CSI Global Education Inc. (2004) Chapter 5 page 5-11
5   CSI Global Education Inc. (2004) Chapter 5 page 5-11

CHAPTER 24

The P.E.P. Principle

Cherish your own emotions and never undervalue them.
– Robert Henri (1865-1929)

Initiating
Conversations

Do you think government politics can affect a person's future financial goals?

How can government economic policies affect a person's standard of living?

Do you know how you might plan for an unforeseen negative financial event?

For about five years I had the privilege of speaking at a high school in my community during their career and personal planning classes on a program I developed called *Fun with Finances*. It was an Introduction to Financial Planning course for grade 11 and 12 students. Over the five years, the course extended from a one-day presentation to a set of 5 presentations to four or five classes each year. Teaching was one of the professions I may have gone into if it wasn't for my choice of a financial planning career so I enjoyed this very much.

Yes. But people often don't understand how.

One learning outcome of the course was illustrating to students how the global stock market reacts differently each and every business day. I had good results in explaining it by what I called the P.E.P. Principle. P.E.P. stands for **P**olitics, **E**conomics and **P**ersonal Emotion.

I have to admit that I am a 'political junkie' and like to follow what is happening politically around the world. I believe that a particular country's **political** views have an influential effect both internally to its own citizens and externally to its trading partners in other countries. The government in power—whether left, right, or in the middle of the political spectrum—will add to a country's legacy, good or bad depending on one's view. Economic decisions can be influenced by what the

Government rules and regulations can affect decisions that you make to create your desired standard of living. governing party views as the right thing to do at the time, which can be added to or corrected when a new government forms. In Canada, if the budget is not passed by the parliament, this is seen as a vote of non-confidence and the government party in power could fall. Therefore, the political landscape in Canada has a big influence on the economic policy of the day.

Economics may seem like a boring subject to most, but it is important to your financial plan. A country's economic outlook each year is reflective on how the stock and bond markets may act going forward, and history is always a good lesson. Monetary policy, tax system, interest rate policy, credit rules, and lending policies, to name a few, all have an effect on how the world looks at a particular country from an investment and bond market perspective. Most people see the economy as the buying and selling of goods, housing prices, and how much money we have left over after each paycheque. The economy of a particular country is often a reflection or a reaction to the same country's government policies.

Personal emotion is one of the few things we can control. It affects your overall financial plan in a number of ways, and it is important to be as pro-active as possible. One of the main aspects of a financial plan where personal emotion is of big concern is in investment planning and risk tolerance. With the world news being available 24/7 by a number of media sources, you often get exposed to more information than you can handle. Information is very important, but so is being able to distinguish what affects your financial plan as it is often hard to know how certain information will affect you personally and therefore uncertainty creeps in.

Risk can bring out a wide spectrum of emotions. You may ask, "Do I like to take risk?", "How much risk is enough?", "What if I lose money?", or you may say, "I only want a guarantee."

After a long working life, retirement is a reward for the many years of hard work. Not knowing what the federal government retirement program will look like can affect the risk taken in investment accounts you may have.

When it comes to choosing a mortgage, one spouse may prefer the variable rate while the other wants a fixed rate. When it comes to retirement, both spouses want to retire at age 60 and travel, but one lives for today and the other makes sure there is enough for tomorrow.

One way I like to deal with client emotions is to ask as many questions as needed to earn a level of trust to build upon going forward. A second way is by educating clients in finances as the relationship develops as I have found it builds a comfort level as each client becomes more used to the financial lingo, makes time to review what has happened so far in their financial plan, and sees the importance of planning to assist in meeting their financial planning goals during their working years to retirement years.

Be as pro-active as possible in your financial plan so that times of re-action are minimal.

Sharper

Focus

- Ask your grandparent's or a friend's grandparent's how economics and politics in their lifetime have affected the financial decisions that they made.

- Ask your parent's what lessons they learned from their parent's in regards to emotions about money.

- Ask a friend about what they learned from their family about economic times during their lives so far.

CHAPTER 25

Open Up Wide

Trips to the dentist – I like to postpone that kind of thing. - **Johnny Depp**

Initiating
Conversations

Is it better to put appointments off in life or tackle the issue right away?

Have you been able to make the necessary changes to fill any 'financial cavities'?

When is your next financial check-up?

Which phone call would you pick up, a call from your dental office to book your regular check-up or a call from your financial planner's office to book your regular review? You may look to postpone both, but you know that both appointments are important to book.

I have always believed that there is something missing when it comes to how people view financial planning. People schedule doctor and dentist appointments, but often don't view a financial planning appointment as important to their health. I often have wondered if you should be able to take time off work once a year to have your annual financial planning check-up just as you would to see your doctor or dentist. I would argue that an employee that keeps his or her health in check as well as their finances would increase productivity. Getting rid of financial stress in society is very important. But these days, time off from work costs the employer money and benefit plans are not the cheapest. So in a busy society can you make time for your regular financial planning check-up?

Ever since I was five or six, I have gone to the same dental office for my regular check-up and made the no-cavity list many times. A few faces have changed over

One financial cavity at a time.

the years with the original dentist, Dr. Mah, retiring and Dr. Hui taking over, and unsurprisingly, technology has changed (and I like to ask questions on what is new), but care of the patient has continued to be the number one priority. I always dread when I get the check-up call. Not that I don't like to go, but rather that I am going to be nicely reminded by Dr. Hui and Hygienist Joanne that I really need to focus more on everything that they teach me, as the proof is in my mouth that I don't. I always give the excuse that I don't have enough time in the morning and at night to do more than a regular brush. I guess they could always point to the poster in the waiting room that says, "Only floss the teeth you want to keep."

So I thought I would use the example of a visit to the dentist to outline what could be reviewed if you were to go to a financial planning check-up.

The Chart – History of work done and decisions that were made in the past for reference. Just like your dentist, your financial planner should keep your file up to date not only with copies of the work that was completed, but also notes from your discussions so you can review why or why not certain decisions were made.

One financial cavity at a time.

The Questionnaire – If you ever had to fill out a new patient questionnaire from a financial planning perspective you would most likely let your planner know about your risk tolerance and any past investment or financial planning 'cavities', any history of financial planning work that has been done before with other advisors, and anything that you would like to accomplish as a starting point.

Hygienist Joanne

The Cleaning, Scaling and Polishing – One thing that you just can't do during a cleaning appointment is talk much, but it is a great time to listen to Joanne explain what is happening with my tooth health so I can improve my habits. Scaling the plaque from your teeth is similar to taking all the bad spending habits out of your budget to improve your cash flow each month.

Fluoride – Having extra resistance to tooth decay sounds perfect to me! Your financial planner can give you that extra expert information that can help you anticipate potential financial steps backward that are easy to make between appointments and instead make positive decisions to get you ahead until your next check-up.

Regular Care – Just like you should brush and floss your teeth on a regular basis, you should also keep track of your budget and cash flow habits. You should keep your statements, tax returns, and pension statements to bring to a future check-up. If things get too sensitive, like buying toothpaste dedicated to helping you with tooth or gum pain, you should talk to your planner to create a sensitive budget until things feel better. Fighting the risk of having a cavity or gum disease can be similar to making sure you keep your financial plan risk free as much as possible and protecting your ability to maintain your standard of living by having a disability plan, a life insurance policy, an emergency fund, and positive budgeting and cash flow care.

Dr. Hui

Cavities and Fillings – I don't know anyone who enjoys having a cavity filled, but it does happen, and it is best to get it filled sooner than later. Dr. Hui makes

I'll be pro-active and give my financial planner a call.

it as painless as possible for me, as he does for all his patients. A financial plan is often not 'cavity free'—either due to actions of your own (over spending, taking too much investment risk) or by uncontrolled actions (losing a job, having an accident). The sooner you work with your financial planner to make some 'financial fillings', the better you will be over the long term. Having the assistance of a financial planner is often better than trying to fill your financial cavities with the wrong filling solutions. Just like Dr. Hui explains the processes to me as each filling step is done, your financial planner does the same for you. To me, knowledge adds comfort to any situation you face.

Root Canal – Saving a tooth could be similar to tactics to save your financial plan if the fillings don't work on the first try. For whatever reason, if something goes wrong, your financial planner can create some solutions to ease the financial pain you are going through. I have been lucky enough not to need a root canal, but I know from others that it is an experience they would prefer not to have again. A perfect financial plan would be to do what is needed to not have to go through a financial root canal. There may be times that you can't control the outcome so a financial root canal may be necessary.

Questions – Just like your dentist and hygienist, your financial planner is always there to answer any questions that you may have, as they are professionals that you can rely on. What might seem like something insignificant to you may have a great impact on your future health—whether it is from a tooth and gum perspective or from a financial planning perspective.

Follow-Up – If you do have to come back before you next scheduled review, it is always best to make the appointment before you leave, as if you don't, you will most likely conveniently 'forget' about it until your next check-up. This can be detrimental to your overall health and create unnecessary issues in the future that could have been prevented. Your financial planner does his or her best work when they have a client that is going to be involved in their own financial well-being. I encourage you to do your part.

Sharper Focus

You only know if your plan needs to be updated if you ask questions and have scheduled reviews.

- If you don't have a financial planner, ask your friends, family, and colleagues for a referral and make an appointment.

- If you do have a financial planner, when is your next check-up? Schedule it today and create a list of questions to ask.

- Ask your employer if you are able to take a few hours off each year to visit your financial planner. Financial well-being will make you a more effective employee!

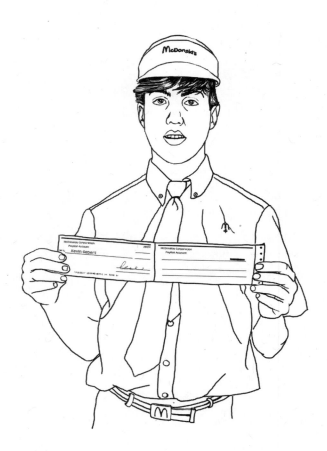

CHAPTER 26

Spend or Save: Cash Flow and Net Worth

The three most dreaded words in the English language are 'negative cash flow'. - David Tang

Initiating Conversations

Why is your net worth important to know and build upon?

Do you remember a lesson learned when growing up regarding your variable expenses?

Would you save more or pay off debt if you received a raise?

Cash flow and net worth are, on one hand separate entities, but on the other hand, they are related. Separate in the sense that each creates a unique financial statement, and related because your decision on how you work with your cash flow can be one of the variables that will potentially increase your net worth.

The word *budget* is often used instead of *cash flow* when discussing financial planning, but one of the major contributors to your cash flow statement is the income that you receive, whether it is from earned income or income from your retirement plans (i.e. income can also come from investments and property).

So that the financial decisions you make can be measured through your working and retirement years.

Your net worth statement is a calculation of all your assets and liabilities at a certain point in time. The growth of your net worth over your life will have a major impact on what your retirement and estate plan will look like.

Outside of asset growth (home, investments), the way you organize your cash flow is important in order to create a positive (spend less than you bring in) cash flow situation for as long as possible. If you have a month or two of negative cash flow, you will have to review your income sources and your spending and saving habits.

Cash Flow Statement

Income Statement

Income Type		Gross	Net
Spouse Employment			
Part-Time Work			
Spouse Employment			
Part-Time Work			
Business			
Alimony / Support Payments			
Pension			
Investment			
Total			A

Questions:

- Does your income fluctuate during any pay periods each year? How?

- Is your work subject to any seasonal changes or layoffs? How?

- Do you receive any income increases or raises during the year? When and how much?

- Do you expect any special payments in the next year? Inheritance or start of pension?

- Are you aware of any other major change or life event that will occur in the next 6-12 months that will create a need to review your cash flow statement?

Monthly Expenses	Allocation ($)	Monthly Expenses	Allocation ($)
Housing		**Insurance**	
Rent or Mortgage		Life	
Property Taxes		Disability	
Utilities / Maintenance/Upkeep		Critical Illness	
Food		Long Term Care	
Groceries		Health	
Meals Away from Home		Mortgage	
Personal		Homeowner	
Medical/Dental/Health Care		Vehicle	
Education/Memberships		**Debt Payment**	
Transportation		Credit Card_____	
Car Loan / Lease		Credit Card_____	
Maintenance/Repairs/Parking/Plates		Line of Credit _____	
Gas/Fuel		**Investment**	
Public Transportation		RSP	
Entertainment		Savings	
Entertaining / Restaurants		Other _____	
Vacations		**Total**	B
Hobbies, Interests			
Other _____			
Clothing			
Other _____			
Miscellaneous			
Gifts			
Professional Fees			
Alimony Support			
Household Help			
Childcare			

Use these worksheets to create your monthly net cash flow. Once completed, take your *total net income (A)* and subtract it from your *total monthly expenses (B)* to total your net positive or negative cash flow (A-B= +/- cash flow). You can find a version you can download at www.financialfotographs.com

As you fill out the expenses portion, you will have fixed expenses (items you need to have) and variable expenses (items you don't need every month). You have your hands tied with most fixed expenses, but there could be a few changes you can make. With variable expenses, you will need to prioritize to see what changes can be made. The best option to create a posi-

When I worked in the mall, I would occasionally spend as much as I made at my store since we received employee discounts.

tive cash flow would be to bring more money in each month, but that is not always possible. Remember to treat yourself once in a while as a reward for keeping your cash flow up to date.

Net Worth Statement

Investment Assets	Amount	Personal Use Assets	Amount
RSP / RRIF		Personal Residence	
Savings		Household Items	
GIC		Vehicles, Boats	
Life Insurance Policy Values		Hobby Equipment	
Non-Registered Investments		Jewelry and Other Valuables	
Investment Properties		Art and Antiques	
Business Interests		Other _____	
Vested Company Pension		Other _____	
Other _____		Other _____	
Other _____		**Total Assets**	
		Liabilities	**Amount**
		Mortgage	
		Bank Loans	
		Credit Cards	
		Line of Credit	
		Other _____	
		Total Liabilities	
		Total Assets	
		Subtract: Total Liabilities	
		Net Worth	

Building your net worth is a vital part of your overall financial plan during both your working and retirement years. If you are not increasing your net worth, then your retirement lifestyle will most likely not meet your expectations. Paying down debt is one of the main aspects of increasing your net worth, with your mortgage being one of the biggest debts you will have in your lifetime. Keeping track of your net worth quarterly or semi-annually is a good start. Working with your financial planner is important in order to create a net worth plan that is relevant to you today and in the years ahead.

Pay off debt, but it depends on the amount of debt, the interest rate I am paying on the debt, and the potential growth of my investment.

Many people keep statements—opened or unopened in envelopes, in a shoebox, or in a binder—but they don't keep a running total. Keeping track of your cash flow and net worth statements may not be the most enjoyable activity, but it is an increasingly important one as you build your wealth and grow in your chosen career. Knowing what your cash flow and net worth statements say will create opportunities to make financial adjustments on a regular basis so that you can create a standard of living you deserve and a retirement that you will enjoy.

Sharper Focus

- Dedicate time each month to collect all of your income statements and receipts to create or update your monthly cash flow statement. Keep a printed copy in a binder or saved on your computer.

- In the next month, collect all the information regarding your assets and liabilities to create or update your net worth statement.

- Give your parents or a friend a call to see how they have handled their cash flow and net worth throughout their lives. If they don't keep their own statements up to date, set a mutual goal to get them done in a month and meet for a coffee to celebrate.

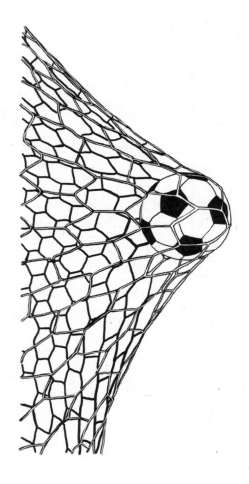

CHAPTER 27

Goals and Priorities

The key is not to prioritize what's on your schedule, but to schedule your priorities. Stephen R. Covey

Initiating
Conversations

What is important to you in regards to your financial well-being?

Why is your financial well-being important?

Why is it important to prioritize your goals?

I was lucky in my early years to be a part of some successful soccer teams. One goal my team achieved was qualifying to represent British Columbia for our age group at the Canadian Championships in Ontario. Back then a 12-month soccer season was the norm. If we weren't playing in our regular season, we were practicing or playing teams a couple of years older. My position was left wing, as I was able to kick well with both feet, and I scored a few goals. But even at a young age there was a position competition each week, so my personal goal was to remain in the starting 11. Each player on the team had a different role to play, but we all had a common goal to win. In order to attain this goal, we had to prioritize, and usually spending time with friends lost out to soccer. But it wasn't that bad, as we all loved being on the pitch and with this particular team it was the most success I had in soccer.

Providing for my family and being able to give them a few things I missed out

When you work with a financial planner you probably don't need a team of 11 players, but your advisor is like your coach for your financial plan. Your planner has to assemble a team with different positions and expertise so that your goals and priorities are met within your financial game plan. Your team should start with positions such as lawyer, accountant, mortgage broker, realtor, and others that complement the specialized needs you have within your financial plan. As your financial plan changes, so should the members of your team.

For example, if you take your monthly budget and write down your fixed costs (i.e. mortgage, rent, groceries, and utilities) and variable costs (premium TV channels, vacation, entertainment, eating out) you will need to prioritize your budget goals for the month. Fixed costs are difficult to prioritize, as they need to be paid, but you will need to learn to prioritize your variable costs. Some months each variable cost might need to be adjusted simply due to the fact that there is not enough money to go around. Going into debt to pay for all variable costs should not be an option you consider.

One of my first goals after my wife and I were married was to buy our first home. It was a goal that wasn't fulfilled until we were married for about eight years, but we were diligent in scheduling a list of our priorities to get to the date we signed the papers and received the keys to our home. There was hard work with some sacrifices along the way, but it was well worth it. I don't think we could afford our house today. You will find that sometimes in your life that certain decisions that were made and goals that were accomplished will be of the 'perfect place, perfect time' variety.

So that I can show my children skills that they can pass down to their family.

Everyone has different goals and priorities, but a few common themes do emerge. Below is a list of ideas that will help you start the conversation about financial goals and priorities with your family. Take out a piece of paper and write down those that are common with you and add goals that you want to or need to work towards.

Living
- finding a place to rent
- buying your home
- moving to a retirement home

Lifestyle
- buying a big ticket item
- planning for a vacation
- growing your assets

Family
- having a child
- caring for parents
- saving for children's education

Home
- qualifying for a mortgage
- renovating
- finding vacation property

Career or Business
- creating a business model
- going to school to upgrade marketable skills
- changing jobs

Taxes
- finding different ways to save tax
- searching for tax efficient investments
- planning to lower estate taxes

Retirement
- deciding when to retire
- making decisions on your retirement lifestyle
- plan today so that you will hopefully have lower taxes during retirement

Legacy Planning
- creating an estate plan
- planning charitable giving
- updating your will and power of attorneys

Anxieties
- defining your investment risk tolerance
- protecting your ability to earn an income
- ensuring enough money is saved

You have a better chance of being successful.

Once you have made your list of goals and priorities to discuss, you need to flesh it out with additional detail. As you revisit your list, do the following:

- prioritize goals under each section
- add additional steps to achieve goals if needed
- add a realistic date to meet each step and the final goal
- figure out how much money you need to save
- find a professional who will help you meet your goal
- determine how goals you meet today will affect future goals

Sharper Focus

- Ask your parents about the financial goals they had when they were at the stage of life you are at currently.

- Sit down with your spouse or partner and create your list of goals and priorities together.

- Sit down with your friends and have each of you create a separate list and discuss both the similarities and differences to learn from each other.

CHAPTER 28

Fun with Files, Envelopes, or Whatever You Have

Electricity is really just organized lightning. – **George Carlin**

Initiating
Conversations

Do you have an easy time getting ready to prepare your taxes?

What do you prefer to do to keep track of your monthly receipts and bill payments?

Are you organized enough to be able to follow a budget each month?

Everyone paints a picture in their mind of what an organized life would look like. What looks like an organized life to one person could mean chaos to another. An organized *financial life* can also mean different things to different people.

If you put all your receipts into an envelope, would that define organization to you? When making a payment, would you feel organized if you robbed 'Peter to pay Paul'?

"Only if I am organized."

Organization in your financial world can be a key factor to lowering your overall stress level. It means knowing where all your current statements are and having them easily accessible if needed at a moment's notice. It means reviewing your financial statements even if you don't fully understand them. It means opening all of your mail to ensure you don't miss an important bill or notice and get charged for late penalties and interest charges. It means compiling and organizing your monthly spending information in a tool like a spreadsheet and not stuffing all of the paperwork in the kitchen drawer.

A great way to get organized is to buy an accordion filing system or set up monthly files in a filing cabinet where you can sort all of your

I use an Excel spreadsheet. financial paperwork on a monthly basis: receipts, bank statements, bills, and pay stubs. Make sure to also include your tax returns so that you have your tax information (including RRSP room, Capital gain and loss summaries etc.) at your fingertips for review. This organized system will set you up to keep track of your monthly spending habits. Whenever you're out and make a purchase be sure that you keep your receipt. When you arrive home you can deposit the receipt in the corresponding month and it can be used in the future to track your spending and it's easily available if you have to return something (or need warranty information) you bought.

Also, sort all credit card statements and other paperwork by the month. You can cross reference all your receipts to your monthly credit card statement to make sure you weren't double billed for anything or a credit was applied to your card. If you know what money is coming in and what money is going out you will know your monthly cash flow status.

Once everything is organized for a three or four month period you can then calculate your average spending habits and decide what (if anything) needs to be changed. Over a year you can take into consideration *Physical folders labeled for each month* the costs that occur once or twice a year. We will get into the specifics in later chapters of this book, but getting things together in one place is more than some people actually do. If you are disorganized then you may realize too late that what is going out in spending each month is more than the money coming in. Then the vicious debt cycle will start.

Sharper Focus

- Ask your family and friends how they keep themselves financially organized (or disorganized).

- Figure out an organizing system that will work for you and stick with it.

- Find a safe and secure storage place for all tax information for future reference.

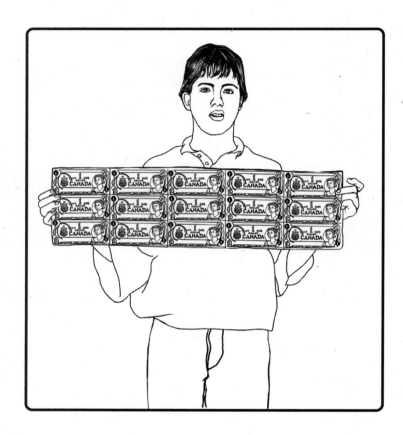

CHAPTER 29

Money In and Money Out

He that, when he should not, spends too much, shall, when he would not, have too little to spend. - **Feltham**

Initiating
Conversations

What is the first thing you remember buying with the money you earned from your first job?

Would you pay yearly rather than monthly for a product or service if you saved money doing it?

Do you know what you are charged for on your cable or phone bill each month?

As soon as I was old enough to babysit, I spent most of my Friday and Saturday nights earning enough money to save up and buy the newest Atari 2600 game. Whether it was Pitfall, Chopper Command, Pressure Cooker, or my favorite, Enduro, my goal was to beat the required high score. If I was successful, I sent away a picture of the television screen showing the high score to Atari headquarters and a few weeks later I received a badge in the mail. *Atari 2600* A goal accomplished and on to saving my babysitting *video game.* earnings for the next game.

A few years into my babysitting gig, I turned 16 years old and according to my parents it was time to get a job as my next goal was to buy a television and VCR for my room. McDonald's wasn't on the top of my list of job opportunities, but I remember deciding to go to my very first interview as it seemed everyone at my high school was getting a job there. The job interview wasn't as stressful as I thought, and soon after I was hired. The best two parts of my job were that I had more money to spend earning $3.15 per hour (this did seem like a lot of money to me at the time) and, of course, free food. I also learned the people skills necessary to succeed in business.

A couple weeks after my first shift I brought home my first cheque and guess what...my mom was there with her camera to document the event. The picture captured me in my nice uniform along with a sarcastic smile. It was great to get money on a consistent basis that I could spend on my own with no worries in the world. No rent to pay, no budget to keep track of—just money to spend. This was made possible because everything else was provided by my parents as long as we were in school full time. We only needed to find our own spending money. For me, this was courtesy of the 'Golden Arches' and later a store in the local mall selling sportswear and shoes.

Unfortunately, I didn't learn much about the importance of saving for the future as it wasn't discussed in our family, and it wasn't part of my high school curriculum that I can remember.

One thing I can remember is my dad sitting down at our kitchen table helping me complete my very first paper tax return. I'm not sure if my dad knew that his helping me was teaching me an important financial lesson in itself (and actually creating RSP room for me to use in the future) on the importance of tax returns! I wasn't making close to my personal exemption but this activity (fun that it is) set the stage for every tax year going forward

As everyone's spending habits are different, it is very important to keep track of where your money goes. One regular question I heard from my mom growing up and now hear from my wife is "where did my money go?" after returning from the grocery store with the groceries.

Yes, only if I don't have to borrow money to do it.

Just like keeping track of the items you need on a grocery list to help you stay focussed at the grocery store, it is just as important to be aware of all your spending habits and track what money comes in and what money goes out each month. Out of control spending habits are the start of debt problems down the road. These debt problems can start very quickly and compound even quicker. Even though it may seem to be a pain to keep track of everything you spend, it will help you in the short-term by drawing attention to bad spending patterns and teaching you what spending habits work best for you; therefore benefiting you and your family in the long-run.

The payment method—cash, debit, or credit card— you use to purchase your groceries and other needs and wants depends on your comfort or stress level. If you use cash or your debit card, the money is removed from your account right away. If you use a credit card, it is much easier to defer worrying about paying for your purchases until you receive the statement in the mail and find you may not have the money in your savings or chequing account to cover what you owe. Without keeping track of your spending habits your credit card statement will always be bigger than you had planned.

If you go to the *Financial Fotographs* website (www.financialfotographs.com) you can download a cash flow statement that assists you in putting pen to paper and comparing your cash flow to future or past months. It is good to find the average for your fixed and variable expenses in case there are any increases or decreases in certain months each year (just like your income could change in certain months). To do this, take the time to fill out the monthly form using the information that you have gathered for the past month. After adding everything up, you will see if you have a shortfall or surplus. You may find it valuable to calculate a percentage for each category so that you can see how each one compares to the others within your overall spending pie. You could then use this as a financial conversation starter to compare to your family and friends or Canadian statistic information comparing fellow Canadians in different parts of Canada or at certain income and net worth categories. You won't know if you are doing well if you can't compare your monthly numbers to someone else's. You can't prioritize your spending habits if you don't keep track of what you spend your money on. You may be surprised by what you see. You may be setting the trend, a good trend I hope!

Sharper
Focus

- Engage in a conversation with your friends and family about their regular payday splurges. Are they surprised by how much they spend on these indulgences?

- Create a cash flow statement with your child using their allowance.

  - Are they saving up for something special?

  - How long will it take to reach their goal?

  - How do they spend their money?

  - Do they have a surplus or a shortfall?

- Search the internet to find Canadian Statistics that will help you have some numbers to compare your monthly and yearly numbers to.

CHAPTER 30

Movin' the Ducks Around

A penny saved is a penny earned. - **Benjamin Franklin**

Initiating
Conversations

When you were growing up, did your parents have a budget that they followed?

Do your friends or siblings follow a budget in their adult years?

Would you be willing to change your spending habits around if it saved you money?

In the chapter "Money In and Money Out", you had the task of keeping track of all your income sources and expenses over a period of a couple months. The more you complete, the better, but one month is a great start! This is the first step in creating a budget. The idea of a budget is not all that exciting, but it is a tool that helps you get closer to your financial planning goals and objectives quicker than you may think.

As I develop a budget with clients, I like to use the illustration of equating budget items to ducks. If you move them around into certain formations, you can discover a way to have things move more smoothly each month and hopefully save some money. It's usually easier said than done at first, but as the months roll on it tends to get easier. I bet that everyone feels better once the money they make is actually benefiting them rather than paying off the interest on the 28% credit card.

Money in is basically all the money that you receive on a monthly basis. This can consist of your earned income or money that you receive from your investments on an after tax basis. Any raise is a benefit, but it is not always realistic. When a raise comes along or any other consistent income increase occurs, you have to make the decision to either increase your spending at the same level of your increase or to use that increase to meet a bigger goal quicker than planned, such as savings or debt re-payment. You have to remember that a realistic amount of

inflation needs to be added to your budget expenses each year. Like the air that we breathe, you can't see inflation but it does occur. Unless you increase the money allocated to pay your expenses, you will end up getting less with the money that you spend.

When reviewing your budget, it is always a good strategy to consider options to pay bills with an annual payment if it will save you money. It may take a year to prepare your finances to do this, but once you are there it is a great idea. Once you can pay some expenses with an annual payment, you should still list these expenses (e.g. house insurance, car insurance, life insurance premiums) as a monthly expense and put the funds into savings so that you are not borrowing the money when the yearly bill is to be paid. Just don't spend this money until your specific annual expenses are due!

Even though a budget is organized to place similar themed costs together under categories, you need to distinguish between your fixed and variable expenses. *Fixed expenses* are things that you need to spend on

Don't know. I should ask them.

a monthly basis and you can't really live without. Examples of fixed expenses are your hydro bill, food bill, and your rent or mortgage. There will be others, but it is important to highlight the expenses that you need to maintain that are essential to your daily living. You may even classify some expenses that you feel are fixed costs, but would usually be defined as variable expenses. *Variable expenses* are those costs that you could live without or you don't need every week or every month—cable, eating out, a regular vacation, for example. It is easy to see every expense as a fixed expense if it is necessary to maintain the standard of living you are used to. But, in the end, your standard of living is partly defined by the items you can afford and if you can't afford them on a regular basis, you need to re-define your standard of living. When you list variable expenses, it is important to list them in order of necessity or what is most important to you if you could only choose a couple of variable expenses each month.

The topic doesn't come up

A big portion of everyone's budget is debt repayment—in particular, a mortgage, credit cards, and vehicle loans. It is important to determine how you will pay down your debt as soon as possible so that your interest costs will lower and the money going to debt and interest can start going towards your spending needs or retirement planning sooner. One method of paying down your mortgage sooner is to pay bi-weekly instead of monthly instalments so that you get in a few extra payments per year. However, you need to make sure that you don't go outside your means when paying down your mortgage as you never want to use credit cards to cover your 'money out' shortfalls. Credit cards are a valuable tool to build up your credit rating, but only if you are paying the balance owed in full each month. In regards to a vehicle loan, you may find it better to get a loan from your bank rather than financing through the car dealership. Or, it may make sense to consider leasing your vehicle depending on the work that you do.

If you are in a debt position with credit cards and other loans, you should pay down the minimum on each debt and then look to the one or two that have the highest monthly or yearly interest charges and pay those down with any extra money you can afford. If you have a $10,000 debt charging you 7% per year and a $500 debt charging you 30% per year, you need to pay more than the minimum on the one with the highest **interest cost** and not just the highest interest rate. This could change each month, so you need to keep track and hopefully be able to pay off each debt in full as soon as possible. It might make you feel better if you pay off the smallest balance first, but in the end, you want to pay off your total collective debt in full while paying the lowest amount of interest possible - mo*vin' the ducks around*.

As a last resort, you can look to your mortgage lender as a source of money if you have enough equity in your home and the lender is willing to take all or many of your debts and pay them off with a consolidation loan. This is usually at a lower rate than your average credit card, but you need to read the fine print before you agree to do anything. You could also shop for lower interest credit transfers with another credit card company, but you have to be careful and find out if there are any balance transfer fees, the length of the temporary rate with the new card before it goes back to the standard rate, and how much interest you will save in the end without having to pay another balance transfer fee to another card and start the whole cycle again.

It is always a rewarding feeling when you meet your financial planning goals, whether you are just setting and following your budget for a couple months or paying a certain amount of money against your mortgage.

Yes. Of course.

Sharper

Focus

- Is there an item in your budget that you can do without?
- Find one or two items in your monthly budget that can be items included only quarterly.
- Are there a few fixed costs in your budget that should really be variable costs?

CHAPTER 31

The Interview

To be on a quest is nothing more or less than to become an asker of questions. - **Sam Keen**

Initiating
Conversations

What types of questions did you ask your first financial advisor before you decided to work with him or her?

What are some good ways to find an advisor?

How do you know that you have made the right decision in choosing a financial advisor?

Like a good pair of shoes you also want to find a good fit when searching for a financial planner. It may not be the most enjoyable task, but it is a very important decision that you will be making. You want to make sure that you make the right choice for today and beyond. You need someone that you can put your trust in to assist you in meeting, and hopefully exceeding, your financial planning goals and objectives.

One of the first steps that you should take is to ask your family, friends, and co-workers for a referral. As everyone's situation is different, it is good to select at least three financial planners to interview. Don't be afraid to ask the tough questions, as you need to know if the person you choose will make a good fit for you and your family's financial situation.

Top questions to ask:

What are your qualifications? Are you required to follow any regulations?
A financial plan is a process you go through and not a product that you can buy. It is important that you ask for confirmation of the qualifications (e.g. CFP designation) and licenses that that your potential advisor holds. There may be a specialty that you are looking for and

want to know if the advisor has experience and training in this area. There are many designations available for advisors to achieve in the marketplace, so it is important that you ask for explanations on what each educational achievement means and how it could help you if you became a client of the advisor.

Ask the prospective advisor which provinces and territories they are registered in. If you are planning to move to a different part of Canada in the future, this registration information should be an issue to discuss beforehand. You wouldn't want to put together a financial plan and then find out you will need to find another advisor who is located where you are moving to due to advisor registration issues.

What is your experience and education?

A financial planner could have started their career working towards their designations or may have achieved it after being established for some time. The advisor may have entered the industry right out of high school or after working 20 years in a different industry. Education and work experience are a good fit together. Some financial advisors start out as a junior advisor in a bigger planning firm, work as an employee at a financial institution, or start out on their own as an independent advisor.

Experience, education, ethics and how the advisor was paid.

As planners have different amounts of experience, it is important to find out where they will get the answers to your financial planning questions and needs if you become a client. If they use other experts, then that should be a positive rather than a negative. You can't expect your advisor to know the answer to every question you have. It is best to find a planner that you feel comfortable with, who will meet your needs, and will have the resources available to refer you to other professionals.

What is your code of ethics and requirements for continuing education?

The FPSC (Financial Planning Standards Council) sets out regulations, code of ethics, and continuing education requirements that each planner needs to abide by to renew their registration each year. Other designations the advisor may hold should have similar requirements, but it is always good to ask up front. Ronald Regan once said to "trust, but verify", so don't be afraid to ask for this information in hard copy to verify, as trust is earned not automatically given.

What is the background of the firm you work for?

Ask the advisor about the background of the firm they work for. Will you be a client of the firm or the advisor, or is the advisor independent? Also, ask the advisor if there could be any bias or conflicts of interest in a potential client relationship.

Referrals from family and friends, the internet, and financial association websites.

Although it is important to be working with a planner who is part of a firm that you feel comfortable with, I have always believed in 'person' first and 'firm' second. When I first started in the business I was registered with a smaller firm that few knew about. I soon realized it was me that my clients were buying. Clients trusted me and therefore trusted that I had made a wise decision in the firm that I chose to work for. I have heard many stories of frustration from new clients about how they never knew which advisor they would be seeing on each visit to their advisor's firm. They wanted consistency.

Ask the potential advisor a question regarding the administration of your investments. For example, if the firm was to close, what happens to the investments that the advisor looks after? This will either give you further comfort or create additional questions you should ask.

If the advisor is not able or willing to give you this information, you should reconsider hiring them as your potential advisor.

What services and products do you offer?

Ask the advisor about the scope of products and services they are able to offer you. Some advisors only offer you a complete financial plan after which you will need to find another advisor to purchase products to meet your established financial planning goals and objectives. Other advisors are independent and not tied to company branded products, while others are only able to offer a particular number of products. You may also find an advisor that can offer you proprietary products that could be solutions that would meet your needs that you can't find at any other firm. Does the advisor have experience in working with new clients or only experienced investors? Do you want a planner to be familiar with integrating your pension plan with your overall financial plan? Other planners, although able to offer a wide

A comfortable feeling that the advisor will help you meet your goals and good references from the advisor.

range of services, may only focus on estate planning and pension planning. It is important to find a planner that can offer you the services you need.

What is your approach to financial planning?

A planner's approach to financial planning may be built on the type of company they work for or the type of services they are able to offer. The approach could also depend on how the advisor gets paid for the services offered. You could work with a planner who is a generalist (like a doctor who is a general practitioner) who would bring in other experts to assist in the development of your financial plan, or you could work with a planner who focuses in a specific area such as debt consolidation, portfolio management, estate planning, or business planning.

How will I pay for your services?

There are a few different ways for an advisor to get paid for their services. A few examples could be commission only, salary only, combination of commission and salary, fee-for-service, or percentage of assets under management. You need to find a financial planner with the qualifications and experience you desire along with a compensation structure that you feel meets your financial planning needs today and into the future. Depending on the size of your assets, the needs of your situation, and the ongoing work that will be needed, a planner should be able to disclose the approximate costs involved in your potential client relationship. Don't only ask for the annual percentage cost, but also the equivalent dollar cost. The costs should be disclosed in your planner and client agreement upon agreeing to work together.

How have you reacted to past market volatility or client situations?

As a planner will be working with you in different areas of financial planning, it would be a good idea to ask questions regarding situations where the advisor helped clients get out of bad financial planning situations, how the advisor was pro-active with client portfolios in rough patches in the stock market, and how he or she helped a client get out of debt. Depending on the experience and qualifications of the planner, you could get examples that would be a great asset to have in your decision process of picking the right financial planner.

Are there any references I could have?

I always include my resume with my introduction materials as I view an interview with any prospective client as a job interview. It is important to always ask for at least three references that you could contact directly: one client that has recently become a client of the advisor, one client that has been with the advisor for a long time, and one client that is in the same situation as yourself. When contacting these references it is important to ask why they decided to work with the planner, what they like about the experience so far, and what are the financial goals that the planner has helped them achieve.

Sharper Focus

- If you are looking for a financial planner ask a friend or family member who their advisor is and why they decided to work with him or her.

- If you are happy with your financial planner make a note to talk to your friends and family about why they should work with your planner.

- Search for Canadian financial planning websites for additional questions to ask while interviewing a financial planner that you may want to work with.

CHAPTER 32

Alphabet Soup

When I was having that alphabet soup, I never thought that it would pay off. - Vanna White

Initiating Conversations

> *Is the company an advisor works for more important than the advisor's education and experience?*
>
> *Do you find it hard to understand what all the professional designations mean?*
>
> *Is it important to work with one advisor or many advisors through your working years and retirement?*

While I was growing up, I consumed a bowl or two (or more) of alphabet soup. I don't know the nutritional value I received, but at least I was able to eat and learn the alphabet at the same time!

In the early years of my financial planning career, my business wasn't as busy as I had hoped so I decided to get as much education as possible. If a prospect's decision to work with me came down to experience vs. education, I hoped the education side would weigh in my favour.

> *It comes down to comfort level for the client and advisor.*

By furthering my education over the years I have now begun to offer to change my name from Kevin to Campbell as people continue to make comments on the number of designations I have received which I jokingly call 'Alphabet Soup' and because alphabet soup is made by Campbell's®. In the end I just like to build my financial planning education and pass it on.

The first designation I received was from the Financial Planning Standards Council. The Certified Financial Planner designation (CFP) is the gold standard for financial planning in Canada and around the world. I believed that working towards a financial planning designation would be well worth it even though the term 'financial planner' was not well known at the time. I am happy that I started here, as it has paid many dividends in my business. Many hours of happy studying!

One of the annual requirements to keep my CFP credentials is to complete a certain amount of hours of continuing education. To fulfill this requirement, I have spent time each year working towards other designations that I know would benefit my knowledge base as well as add value to my client relationships.

An aspect of my studies that I have found valuable is being able to pass this knowledge on to my clients. Not everyone wants the detail, but many clients want the 'Coles notes' of what we are discussing. Knowledge often brings comfort to a client when a decision needs to be made. I believe that it is my job to take time in building financial knowledge with my clients while building a financial plan together that will meet their goals and objectives throughout their lifetime and will benefit the generations that follow.

It depends on your financial planning needs and the expertise you require.

My experience with clients is that many don't understand what each designation means or what is required to earn the particular letters. Please refer to the reference section of www.financialfotographs.com for further information.

Sharper Focus

- Ask your financial planner to schedule a financial education discussion into each meeting.

- The next time you interview a financial planner ask the advisor to explain their educational journey to date.

- Ask your financial planner how he or she maintains his continuing education hours.

CHAPTER 33

Letter of Engagement

The hardest thing to understand in the world is the income tax. - **Albert Einstein**

Initiating
Conversations

Do you know the responsibilities of your advisor?

Do you know what your responsibilities are as a client?

Are you able to have specific issues covered in the letter of engagement that are particular to your unique situation?

I went to my son's kindergarten orientation prior to the start of the school year to find out what I was to expect from my son's school in regards to curriculum, parent committees, student experience, and was introduced to the teaching staff and Principal. I soon found out that it wasn't going to be as easy as dropping him off in the morning and picking him up after school. There were 'rules' for the kindergarten parents. We were assured by the staff that everything would be fine—and they were right.

I always ask my advisor to explain.

It was good to know that as a parent I was able to engage with my son's teacher during teacher/parent interviews or if I had a question at anytime. Also, there were progress reports (not report cards) during the year which would give me feedback as to whether my son was meeting expectations and becoming a model student just like his dad was (or thought he was).

The teacher/parent relationship that is formed for the school year is similar to one that is outlined in an engagement letter.

As a financial planner it is my duty to create a letter of engagement between myself and my client so that each of us knows our roles in the financial planning relationship we have agreed to commence. There is no perfect template to follow as there can be many aspects of a financial planning relationship. Therefore, a letter of engagement should be created and updated as needed depending on the timeframe and the scope of the relationship. A letter of engagement is important to complete and you should expect this of your financial planner.

From the perspective of a Certified Financial Planner, I have outlined below what I feel is important to include in a letter of engagement with a financial planner based on information provided to CFP professionals from the Financial Planning Standards Council.[1]

Affiliation of associations and registration information: It is important for the planner to disclose to the client the associations he or she is involved with, the name of the company that holds the registration to offer products, and the provinces/territories that the planner is registered to practice in. The client needs to disclose if there may be any conflicts of interest with the types of products that can be invested in depending on the client's employment or current investment holdings (e.g. Is the client a member of a public company board?).

Ownership of client relationship: It is important for the client to know if he or she is a client of the firm or a client of the individual planner in case the planner leaves the firm in the future. This may be different depending on the products the planner is able to offer the client (e.g. investment products and insurance products as licensing may differ).

Confidentiality: It should go without saying that everything a client discloses to his or her planner is confidential, but it should be stated in writing—especially when other advisors are needed to be called upon

to facilitate more detailed solutions to a client's needs (e.g. financial planner consulting a lawyer, accountant, or mortgage broker for client advice).

Detailed list of services to be offered: A client may need a financial planner for a small request or a more detailed set of needs. Therefore, it

---

[1] Financial Planners Standards Council. www.fpsc.ca

is important to create a list of what the planner will and won't be responsible for in a letter of engagement. If a client's needs change in the future, then a new or amended letter of engagement will need to be completed (e.g. Is the need just for a retirement projection with no products to be sold? Is the planner being used for only the determination of the potential risk of disability and therefore only needs to sell a disability policy?).

Not unless they are disclosed to me.

Disclosure of all assumptions used: The client should request that the planner disclose in writing all the assumptions used when calculating future values. This is important so that the client will understand how the planner came to certain assumptions and will know what needs to be altered in the future given a certain event occurring which makes the original assumption not applicable (e.g. the client originally has a goal of retirement of age 60 with a rate of return projection for all investment contributions of 5% until then. Instead, the client decides to retire at age 55 and wants to take more investment risk to try and make up for the inability to make further contributions between ages 55 and 60).

Timeframe of engagement: It is important to agree upon an engagement timeframe that includes completion date in the future, frequency of updates throughout the year, amount of in-person meetings, and the amount of phone meetings. It is also important for the planner to have a client service response agreement so that the client knows when enquires will be attended to.

Compensation: It is important for the planner to disclose all forms of compensation so that the client knows ahead of time the cost based on the scope of the agreement and what payment options are available. Since there are a number of different compensation models a financial planner may follow, the client needs to know if the planner is remunerated by salary, commission, salary plus commission, assets under management, and if additional remuneration will be received by the planner upon different solutions being implemented to meet goals and objectives through the purchase of different products.

Conflicts of interest: As a financial planner, I always like to know if there are other advisors in the picture when it comes to a client's financial plan. Also, if any referral arrangements are being made between a planner and another professional, this has to be disclosed to the client in advance (e.g. referral fee). This is important regarding the confidentiality of the agreement.

Restrictions on licensing or product offerings: It is important for the financial planner to disclose to the client if there are any restrictions on licensing or product offerings so the client knows what to expect and what limitations the advisor will have in regards to offering solutions to their financial planning needs (e.g. if the planner is going to offer an in-house investment solution for a client, a disclosure document acknowledging the relationship is required to be given to the client prior to the purchase of the particular product).

The letter can be as short or long as needed given a client's unique situation and can be amended as needed.

Client requirements: Only what is known is able to be brought into consideration when making recommendations for a client's situation. Therefore, it is important that the client contact the planner whenever something important—big or small—happens in their life (e.g. loss of job, new dependant, getting married, spouse passes away). What might be a small detail in a client's eyes may make a big impact on what the planner recommends going forward. It is important for the client to pass along financial updates to the planner throughout the year (i.e. notice of tax assessments, RSP room balances, pension adjustments, and both Home Buyers' and Life Long Learning re-payment amounts). A small thing such as timely return of correspondence always makes the planner's service to the client easier.

Use of other professionals: Depending on the solutions that the planner may recommend to the client it may be important to call upon other professionals. If clients look to me for investments and insurance solutions while maintaining a relationship with their current advisor, then it is in their best interest for me to know so that I can take this into consideration when offering solutions. I believe a planner can do the best work for the client only if he or she knows everything that is going on. Working together with a client's current advisors can work well, but the arrangement needs to be disclosed at the beginning of the financial planning relationship.

Termination of agreement: Although both parties will want to have the agreement termination date agreed upon in the beginning, one party may wish to end the agreement early. Parameters should be set in case of this occurrence. If the premature ending is due to a negative experience, a conversation between both parties is recommended in order to allow for clarification and correction of any misunderstanding. This conversation will either lead to an agreement to make the changes needed for the relationship to continue, or both parties will decide to end the relationship and go their own way.

I believe it is a planner's duty to both recommend solutions to a client, as each financial plan is unique to everyone's own situation, and to increase the level of knowledge a client builds during the relationship. Some say too much education is dangerous, but I believe that education will only enhance the relationship between the planner and client and will increase the level of comfort in the solutions that are put before the client. This gives more comfort to the planner that each decision made by the client is an informed decision as the client is better educated as the relationship grows.

Sharper Focus

- Review the relationship you have with your financial planner during your next visit.

- Review your financial planning needs on a regular basis to see if there are any additional requirements you need to work with your advisor on which may alter your current agreed upon relationship.

- Ask a friend or family member what their agreement with their financial planner consists of.

CHAPTER 34

Four Generations

I've got all the money I'll ever need, if I die by four o'clock.

– Henny Youngman

Initiating
Conversations

If you don't have a will yet is it because you don't want to discuss the topic?

Would you find it difficult to be a power of attorney for a friend or loved one?

Do you find it hard to discuss estate planning issues with your friends and family?

Having enough money to live on is important to us all but at the same time each of us has a desire to pass something down to another generation whether it is big or small or whether it has monetary value or is a prized possession. I am sure that my wife will inherit my mother-in-law's shoe collection. At least all the shoes can fit into a few display cases rather than a few closets. A great memory I have to remind me of my great aunt Elsie is sitting in my office. It is a stool she made out of cans and cloth that I used when I was about 1 or 2 years old. It is in great condition. The stool still has my name written on the bottom in her handwriting along with the date when she made it.

Yes, and I don't know if it is worth the cost of getting it done.

When I found a picture of myself when I was about four years old along with my dad, my grandfather, and my great-grandfather I thought that it would be a great illustration to use when financial planners talk to their clients about intergenerational estate planning. Most people may only be looking at one generation or two but a conversation about what is important is a great place to start. Goals and objectives will change in the future as a person deals with family dynamics and their own financial planning results but all I am recommending at this point is to have an initial plan to discuss and then go from there. If you already have a plan in place that will make a financial planners day!

Estate planning may not be the most enjoyable discussion to have as it does involve discussions about death. A more enjoyable way of looking at estate planning is what one generation wants to pass down to the next. Estate planning creates a personal plan that meets your goals and objectives so that others know your wishes if you are unable to make your own decisions in the future.

It is much easier to have a plan for others to follow when it comes to your health and property rather than others to decide what they think you wanted. Also, it is easier to have designated people to take care of your affairs rather than the government making decisions on your behalf.

In my personal financial planning practice I do utilize a team of other professionals that will perform the specific duties needed to fulfill a client's estate planning goals and objectives. My goal is to have the initial conversation with clients and then further the discussions with those specific professionals within my family office or other advisors that a client brings to the table.

Important topics to discuss

To have a will or to die intestate – Having a will enables you to express your wishes which should be the start to any estate plan. If you die 'intestate' then you are leaving decisions up to the appropriate government offices and there is no promise that your wishes will be met. A common excuse I have heard many times is that if you are single with no dependants you don't care much about what happens. Dying intestate creates unnecessary issues for surviving family members and friends even if you didn't have anything to pass along. Also, there would be costs associated with the courts to have decisions made that could have easily been answered in a will.

Yes, but it would be important for me to fulfill my friend's or loved one's wishes.

Incapacity Planning – How do you know for sure that your wishes will be met if you experience physical and mental decline due to the normal aging process? A power of attorney is an answer you could consider. A *power of attorney for property* will define what your attorney can do and not do in regards to decisions that need to be made in relation to your property. A *power of attorney for personal care* will define what your attorney can do and not do in regards to decisions of your personal nature after incapacity. A living will (advance health care directive) provides instructions on the type and level of medical treatment you would like to receive (or not receive) during your incapacity. All rules and regulations should be reviewed with your particular provincial or territorial policies. Make sure you ask the person who you are going to be noting as attorney[1].

Planning your funeral - do you want a funeral or not? How do you want to have your funeral wishes granted? Talking to your family and writing your requests down are always a good way to go within your will.

Charitable goals – passing down a percentage of your assets to your charity of choice can generally be done within your will or in certain circumstances can be completed during your lifetime depending on how you would like to receive the tax credit(s).

Setting up a Trust – A trust offers the opportunity to manage different asset strategies in regards to who is responsible for paying the tax on a specific asset, how the taxes will be paid and when the taxes will be paid.

Yes, but it is a necessary conversation!

Due to tax issues it is important to understand the difference between inter vivos trusts (settled during lifetime) and testamentary trusts (settled at death). A few examples of non-tax uses of setting up a trust would be for minors, spendthrift adult children or to cover disability needs[2].

Death and Taxes – it is important that you understand what the tax implication(s) could be depending on your estate planning wishes. What

---

[1] "Incapacity – planning ahead helps," Invesco, January 2012, https://invesco. ca/publicPortal/ShowDoc?nodePath=/BEA Repository/common/library/PDF/ estate_planning/TEINPL//eBinary

[2] "Trusts – Legal Principles and Common Uses," Invesco, June 2012, https:// invesco.ca/publicPortal/ShowDoc?nodePath=/BEA Repository/common/library/ PDF/estate_planning/TETLPC//eBinary

you think is equal on paper might not be equal from a tax perspective. It is important to understand all the potential tax issues in regards to the proceeds from remaining balances of non-registered investments, RRSP, RRIF, TFSA etc.

Government benefits – the federal government provides a small CPP death benefit payment. You will need to verify the requirements and the process for claims.

Beneficiaries – be sure to review your wishes with your legal professional as there are a number of rules regarding beneficiary designations for division of property, insurance policies and other assets within and outside your will.

Guardian for your minors – It is an important choice for you to decide who would become the guardian of your children if you were to pass depending on your situation (single, married but die in a common disaster). There is extra work that should go into this decision rather than just choosing the person who will be named.

Life Insurance – this is an asset that can either by-pass your estate (named beneficiary) or become part of your estate (estate named as beneficiary) so it is important to discuss your wishes with your financial planner and other estate planning professionals.

Have you known of a family member or friend who did not have their estate planning wishes in order once they became ill or passed away? What was the outcome? Did this make you change your mind for your personal situation?

Do you know of someone who had health issues and did not have a power of attorney in place for their property or health? What was the outcome? Did this make you change your mind for your personal situation?

Many stories are passed from generation to generation. Many assets are passed from generation to generation. Make sure that your wishes are defined so that you are confident that they will be carried through by who you choose. Death and taxes are certain but we often don't know when death will be near or if you know death is near you may not be able to make any changes to your wishes. Therefore, if I can stress any-thing to you as a financial planner please make sure you put the steps in place by getting your will completed, updated or have whatever con-versations you need to have in order to make sure that your wishes are set in place regardless of if it is for this generation or the next.

Sharper Focus

- Make a goal to review your will in the next three months (or get one done today!)
- Talk with your grandparents or parents in regards to their estate planning decision making process.
- Make a list of friends or family that you would like ask to make decisions for you if you are unable to due to incapacity.

CHAPTER 35

Do you want to be my Executor?

A dinner invitation, once accepted, is a sacred obligation.
If you die before the dinner takes place, your executor
must attend. – **Ward McAllister**

Initiating
Conversations

Have you been asked to be an executor before?

Would you want to appoint an individual as executor in your will or have a company look after the duties?

What special tasks would you want to leave to your executor?

As a financial planner, one of my first discussions with a potential client is if they have their will updated. More often than I would like to hear the answer is 'no'. My next comment is usually 'I am glad to hear that you actually have a will and we can work on getting it updated'. The response by my prospect is 'I mean that I don't have a will at all.' All of a sudden my meeting notes are now including a big 'WILL' at the top of the page because in my view a financial plan is not complete without a will. It's often the cost that is prohibiting the process from being be done (at least that is what I am told), but a big part of it is that nobody wants to talk about death. The other reason I ask if a will is completed is because I need to know who will be contacting me in the unfortunate situation of a client dying.

Yes, but my firm did not allow me to accept.

I was never asked by my parent's to be their executor but I had to make sure so I had a conversation with my mom one day to confirm that I was correct. Not a comfortable conversation (about death) but an important one. I was happy to confirm that I wasn't because I don't know that I would like to be someone's executor, however I will always be there to help. Your financial planner is most likely not allowed to be your

An individual for more of a personal feel but I would need to find someone who wants to do it.

executor due to your client relationship and a potential conflict of interest. I believe in collaboration with other professionals in my practice and referring to others with different specialties is what I do.

If I would survey my clients, most of them would have a family member or close friend named as Executor (please ask the person you would like to be executor first. Not a good surprise to have put upon you). You don't have to accept the role of executor so make sure when the time comes that you are ready for it. Often people don't want this job but it is a very important part of someone's overall estate plan. It is important to have the resources in place to carry out the job according to all government rules.

To assist you in the role of executor you can consider hiring a lawyer and an accountant but you may make that decision depending on the complexity of the role.

With every estate being different and the role of executor being an important part in the deceased final wishes I have professionals within my network to assist an executor. It can be a lawyer, notary or an accountant. I have also found a great resource for those who want to explore the thought of doing it on their own but having help along the way or if I get the call saying 'Unfortunately I am up to the plate as executor of my friend's estate'. The firm is Executor Support – Probate and Estate Administration. I would like to thank Gregg Medwid for allowing me to use the Executor's Checklist and I have listed a general review, but look for the actual list on the book's website: www.financialfotographs.com.

Preliminary
- Locate the will, make funeral arrangements and apply for the death certificate.
- Meet with the deceased family, beneficiaries and others to review the will.
- Apply for government benefits and advise all necessary institutions.
- Review financial records and statements so that all information can

be updated and you are aware of all accounts and other important information.

Family Relations

- Do some preliminary family research to see if you are going to have to be involved in any family disputes among beneficiaries or if other professionals will need to be brought in to assist.
- Agree to an update system with the beneficiaries

No special tasks outside of fulfilling my wishes as much as possible.

Identify and Protect the Assets

- Identify and locate the assets of the estate
- Take possession of all valuable assets
- Change locks on the residence if necessary
- Review insurance needs with the appropriate insurance carriers to protect the deceased's belongings
- Determine market value of personal belongings and other assets

Apply for Letters Probate *(if probate is required)*

- Decide whether you want to prepare the documents or if you will require the assistance of another professional
- Search for the will in the wills registry
- Choose a probate registry
- Pay the court filing fee and probate fee

Identify Sources of Income

- Employment Income
- Life Insurance Policies
- Pension Plans, Investment accounts (Registered and non-registered)
- Rental income
- Debts that are owed to the deceased
- Business interests

Close Accounts
- Utilities and other service providers
- Credit cards
- Subscriptions and memberships
- Bank accounts

Pay Debts and Liabilities
- Credit Cards and other service providers
- Funeral, burial and other medical expenses
- Property Taxes, personal loans and mortgages

Income Tax Returns
- Consult with other professionals as needed (ie. Accountant)
- Prepare tax returns and pay any income tax owing
- Request a Tax Clearance Certificate from Canada Revenue Agency

Maintain Detailed Bookkeeping Records
- Keep all receipts
- List all assets and liabilities
- Keep track of all revenue earned by the estate

Distribute the Assets and Proceeds of the Estate
- Wait the required amount of time after probate is finalized
- Advertise a notice to creditors and settle all outstanding debts
- Deliver personal possessions that have been bequeathed
- Receive receipts from beneficiaries after they receive possessions
- Provide detailed accounting records of the estate to beneficiaries.

Sharper Focus

- Review your will to see if you want to change the Executor and contact that person to confirm that they are still willing to take on the role. See if you should appoint an alternative Executor if able.

- If you have been appointed as Executor you should contact that person to see if anything has changed.

- As an Executor you should request that all updates regarding assets, liabilities and other important information is in a place that you know of.

CHAPTER 36

Six Steps

Order and simplification are the first steps towards the mastery of a subject. - **Thomas Mann**

Initiating Conversations

Why is it important to give your advisor all the information that he or she needs?

Why is financial planning not a product that you buy?

Why is it important to update your life events with your advisor?

When I started my financial planning career, I decided that it was important to attain the Certified Financial Planner designation (CFP). It was important to me because if I wanted to call myself a financial planner, I needed to make sure that I had the education as well as the experience behind me as I built my financial *So that a proper* planning practice. *financial plan*

can be written.
Today, financial planning is not regulated in Canada so it is important to make sure you ask your advisor to see what process they will take you through when completing a financial plan. Each advisor may brand the process differently, but it should be the same six step financial planning process that every financial planner goes through. The six steps below are main starting points, and the extra details included will depend on your situation.

The planner and client engagement

When you engage the services of a financial planner you want to establish each of your responsibilities from the start. As each client situation and needs are different, it is important to build the initial agreement to ensure everything needing to be accomplished is defined, while at the same time, making it as fair and realistic for both you and the planner.

Each planner may bring different specialities outside of being a generalist, and therefore any specific agreements need to be itemized so that everyone knows their responsibilities. There are different ways that a financial planner can be compensated so it is important to discuss the way that your planner will be compensated throughout your agreement. It is good to review this agreement on a regular basis to make sure any clarifications or changes that need to be done are agreed upon and that you and your planner are holding up to what was initially promised. The amount of contact and a meeting timetable should also be included.

Gathering data

Your financial planner can only work with the information he or she is given by you. Your planner will request that you bring all important documents to your meetings so that all information is reviewed before any recommendations are made. It is very important to disclose all information about your situation. What may not seem important to you may indeed play an important role in your financial planner's recommendations to you. It is also important to know that all information presented in your meetings with your planner is strictly confidential. It is normal for a financial planner to bring other professionals into the picture to meet all your goals. Any information that is passed along will have your permission first to make sure everything remains confidential. You will be asked to complete a few questionnaires that will give the planner a better picture of your risk tolerance and your individual or family goals and objectives. As information changes or is updated, it is very important to pass it along to your planner as soon as possible. Examples of this could be pension statements, tax returns, and asset and debt updates. You need to let your planner know if there are any specific areas of concern going forward or if there are any limitations you want to impose.

You won't know what products to buy until your financial plan is completed.

Clarify and identify potential problems and opportunities

Now is the time for your planner to take all the information he or she has gathered through the questionnaires, interviews, and other conversations and see if there are any problem areas or opportunities (e.g. your cash flow, net worth, investments and tax returns or assessments) that should be discussed further before your financial plan is developed. Areas that may require specific attention right away could include budget needs, cash flow, net worth, estate planning, retirement planning, pension planning, risk management, taxation, elder care, and any needs of dependants. Any clarification will limit problems or challenges in the future.

Develop your financial plan and present it to you

After your financial planner has taken the time to review the information that has been disclosed, it is now time to sit down and have your planner present his or her recommendations to you. These recommendations would include steps to meet your goals and objectives, how to incorporate your values into the plan and the risk tolerance for your investments. Your advisor will also provide you with projections to see what your financial plan will look like into the future—both short and long term.

Throughout the year, it is ideal to establish regular meeting times for review, with the understanding that if an immediate change is needed, a meeting can be arranged in person or on the phone. As a financial plan is made up of many parts, if one changes, it is important to review any impact on the other parts of your plan.

So that your financial plan can be adjusted accordingly and different strategies can be discussed related to your life event.

Implement your financial plan

A financial plan may be taken care of by your planner alone, or he or she may involve the expertise of other professionals like a lawyer, accountant, or mortgage broker. Your planner may already have these people available to assist in carrying out your goals and objectives, but you are always able to use professionals you already use and trust. It is a good idea to introduce your planner to your professional contacts. When working with other professionals, it is important to establish an agreement on the scope of the relationship and the fees that are going to be paid.

Regular monitoring

As established in your engagement letter, both you and your planner have responsibilities to follow. Your planner is the quarterback of your overall financial plan, and he or she will focus on how your plan is affected by changes in the stock market, tax rules, and market risk throughout the year. You are not off the hook, as it is important for you to inform your planner of any changes in your current situation that may alter the outcome of your goals and objectives already established.

As you can see, the process needs to be completed before you even know what products would need to be looked at to meet your goals and objectives. Just like your will, it is not wise to complete your plan and not look at it again until it is too late to make needed adjustments. The amount of detail within a financial plan is up to you and your planner, as your needs and objectives will change over the years.

Sharper Focus

- Ask a friend or family member what type of financial planning relationship process they go through with their financial planner.

- If you have only used an advisor in the past for specific needs explore the opportunity of working with your advisor in more areas the next time you meet in case your advisor's scope of service has increased.

- If you don't know the process that your advisor is following in your relationship ask for more details during your next review meeting.

CHAPTER 37

Riding the Teeter-Totter

It's sort of like a teeter-totter; when interest rates go down, prices go up. – **Bill Gross**

Initiating
Conversations

> When could I make a spousal RSP contribution?
>
> When should I stop making RSP contributions?
>
> If you are married which spouse should get the biggest tax return?

Many of us at some point in our lives have taken a turn on a teeter-totter. And I am sure you have never thought about income splitting while trying to keep your balance or hoping that the person on the other side doesn't fall off. As a parent I have an excuse to continue to take a turn until my kids are 'too embarrassed' to have their dad around.

When your spouse is not working or when your retirement income projections will create a tax bill you do not want to pay.

How does a teeter totter and income splitting go together? I use it as an illustration when discussing the retirement planning concept of income splitting with many client couples. In order for the teeter totter to stay level both sides need to be equal. So, from an income splitting perspective each spouse on their respective sides of the teeter totter needs to create a retirement income together where each of their taxable income is as equal as possible. That's why the discussion of income splitting is important not just during your 'retirement years' but also as soon as possible in your 'working years'.

During the *early years* of a marriage a couple might not have retirement high on their topics of conversation. Conversations are often about building careers, buying a home and having children. If one spouse has a pension plan there might not be much money left (cash flow and budget) over for RSP contributions. If there is money for retirement planning then each year a decision can be made between a RSP and a Spousal RSP contribution. This might not be an important decision at the time but it will become an important choice in the future once you get a better picture of what the family taxable retirement income will look like.

If you can set the plan in place early on it could pay great benefits to you in the future. I often have curious looks when one spouse gets a tax refund and the other has to pay tax. Then I explain that it is true individually but as a family they received a higher tax return than if they had switched the numbers around. I often get a smile of agreement as the couple fights over who owes who. Current tax legislation is never guaranteed in the future so it is better to plan for today so that you can deal with tomorrow in the best tax situation as possible.

During the *middle years* of marriage a couple might start to discuss the topic of future retirement once in a while. This is where the couple will have hopefully increased their RSP, TFSA, and pension plan values. Now they can work with their financial planner to create a few hypothetical illustrations on what their retirement income is going to look like and where they will be able to split their income.

Each year the couple should work with their financial planner to determine if a RSP contribution today added to their current RSP balance will create a future tax liability that makes sense or not. Would you invest $1 today if you knew that that $1 would create $3 of tax liability in the future? I know that this is a simple example but there is a difference when you go out and buy a RSP without contemplating how it will affect your future retirement plan and when you buy the same RSP with your future financial plan (and tax liability) in mind.

When you are comfortable with the retirement income you have built.

When talking to clients about their *retirement years* I explain that in a general sense when they are both retired, spouses should have as equal amount of income as possible. With multiple types of investments and sources of income during retirement it gets more difficult as the years go on.

With the federal government allowing pension income splitting during retirement it doesn't mean that you stop contributing to spousal RSPs for income splitting as this will accomplish the same as pension splitting. One benefit will be allowing the spousal RSP to be redeemed earlier (make sure that you are aware of the attribution rules) than waiting to the age required to pension split. Something to remember is that the increase of costs and liabilities are pushing more employers to offer Group Registered Retirement Savings Plans (GRSP) and Deferred Profit Sharing Plans (DPSP) instead of pension plans. Therefore, limiting the amount of 'guaranteed' income that you will have during retirement and putting the risk of market growth with the employee, his or her investment decisions will create an increased importance of keeping their financial plan updated.

Income splitting is vital to be considered when planning for retirement (no matter how many years before) due to the federal government's rule of OAS (Old Age Security) claw back if your individual net income is too high. If your income is going to create an OAS claw back you need to decide if you are willing to lose an amount of OAS each year or if you need to make some financial planning changes during your working years. For example, you may decide to not invest in your RSP or a spousal RSP for your spouse and give up the tax deduction you would have received and invest in your TFSA instead (watch the contribution rules).

You should put more focus on how the family can receive the best tax return together.

This is by far not a chapter that explains every income splitting strategy, but gives you a few ideas to discuss with your financial planner to create strategies that will get the most out of your hard work from a tax perspective. As government tax rules change so does your financial planning strategies for today, tomorrow and into the future.

Sharper Focus

- Talk with your parent's or grandparent's about how they have dealt with income splitting during retirement.

- Work with your financial planner to review your current investment statements, pension plan statements and projections on your OAS and CPP income to create possible retirement income tax situations to see if changes need to be made today.

- If neither spouse has a pension plan at work look to your financial planner to show you how a spousal RSP contribution will enable you to income split in the future.

CHAPTER 38

I Need More Than Just a Paycheque!

*Work/life benefits allow companies meaningful ways
for responding to their employees' needs; they can be a
powerful tool for transforming a workforce and driving a
business' success.* – **Anne M. Mulcahy**

Initiating
Conversations

How familiar are you with your group benefits plan?

Have you looked at additional coverage to compliment your group plan at work?

What questions should you ask your benefits specialist?

Benefit packages are often part of the overall remuneration package at work. Often I find that many people don't understand their benefits package, and therefore do not incorporate it together with their personal plan. This involves benefits for health care (life insurance, dental, and medical) and retirement planning (group RSP, deferred profit sharing plan, pension plan).

I don't have one as I am part of my wife's plan.

Having a good health and dental benefit plan at work is important to your overall family financial plan. Understanding the benefits will assist in your overall personal monthly budget so that extra out of pocket expenses are planned for.

Incorporating your retirement benefits at work with your personal retirement plan every year is important so that they work together as one until you have to put them together at retirement.

Pension Plans – If you are lucky enough to have a pension plan at work, it will most likely be either a defined benefit pension plan (DBPP) or a defined contribution pension plan (DCPP). Employee involvement is important for both, but more focus needs to be put with a DCPP. This is because you are responsible for the investment choices, and the value

Not at this time, but maybe in the future as needs change. at retirement is reliant on these choices, as the pension value is subject to how your chosen portfolio performs. Whether you have a DBPP or a DCPP, it is important that you keep your financial planner updated so that your statements can be incorporated into your overall financial plan. Any investment changes to your DCPP will most likely need to be initiated by you, so having your financial planner as part of the conversation is the best way to go. The DBPP required contribution amounts can be changed by your employer depending on how the pension plan assets are performing and that all future liabilities (paying retirees into the future) are being met today and for the required amount of years into the future.

Group Plans – With pension plans being expensive to run, it is likely that your employer offers either a group RSP plan (GRSP) or a deferred profit sharing plan (DPSP). Employee involvement in the investment selection is essential, as the future value of the investments is subject to how the market performs. Therefore, it is important to have your financial planner review your statements as part of your overall plan. It is also a good idea to seek guidance from your group plan advisor. Without proper review, you may find that the risk in your personal investment portfolio is much different than your group plan. Remember that the contribution that your employer makes to your plan is just as important to keep track of as your own contribution you make off of your paycheque.

Life Insurance – Depending on your plan, your group life insurance coverage can be a big or small part of your overall benefits plan. Some plans are geared more for health and dental coverage with a small life insurance top up, and some plans do give the employee a reasonable amount of coverage. If you have health issues, then a group plan is great because you may not be able to qualify for an individual plan. Group plans can change and if you are planning on retiring, then you should ask about your conversion options which would create a personal plan outside of your group plan for a period of time after you retire. If you are combining your group coverage with extra personal coverage to meet your insurance needs within your financial plan, it is important to discuss your group coverage with your financial planner as it may decrease upon attaining a certain age group or change all together if your employer changes the group coverage company.

Is there any way that my plan can meet my goals better?

Health & Dental – Understanding your health and dental coverage is very important as you will have to adjust your budget and spending habits depending on the services you need and how much they are covered under your group plan. Talking with your financial planner will enable you to explore personal coverage that you can apply for to offset any coverage shortfalls that you have within your group plan. Personal coverage is often more expensive than group coverage, but it is best to know what other coverage options are out there.

Disability – Understanding your short and long term disability coverage is a must. Ask questions regarding the definitions of coverage so that there are no surprises when you may need to make a claim in the future. Although personal coverage will most likely be more expensive, there are different ways that you can lower the cost to compliment your group coverage if extra coverage is needed. You will need to have emergency funds available to cover any shortfalls, so it is always good to be prepared. You hope that you will never have to use your work disability plan, but in the event that you do, it's best to have considered all options early.

Critical Illness – There have been more group benefit providers adding critical illness coverage to their employee plans. It is important to review the specific coverages of these plans so that you understand the definitions of coverage, as these definitions can be different than a personal plan you may have.

It is important to keep your financial planner informed of your benefits plan at work so that you can have an integrated family benefits plan rather than two separate plans that in the end could have unnecessary overlap.

Sharper

Focus

- Ask for an updated copy of your group benefit plan at work and set up a time to review this with your financial planner.

- Ask your benefits specialist if you can apply for additional personal coverage above what is part of your group benefits package. This way you can compare benefits and costs to a personal plan outside of your group plan.

- Ask for an updated pension plan or retirement plan statement from work and set up a meeting with your financial planner for review.

CHAPTER 39

Investment Policy Statement

Productivity is never an accident. It is always the result of a commitment to excellence, intelligent planning, and focused effort. – **Paul J. Meyer**

Initiating Conversations

> *How often do you review your investment policy statement?*
>
> *Do you know of other friends and family that have an investment policy statement?*
>
> *How many times has your investment goals changed in your life so far?*

If you are someone who doesn't like much structure in life you may not enjoy going through an activity based on a process. Even if it would be beneficial to you, I am sure you would rather learn the outcome as soon as possible.

I remember my high school Consumer Education class and the section on investing. I really didn't know much about investing, but our project during the class was for each of us to pick a few stocks out of the paper and then monitor the performance of the stocks over the following months to see who would come out on top with the highest stock value. My process in picking out stock names was to choose the ones that were the shortest or longest in name or had a certain stock value. Not much of a process other than pure luck.

Reviewing your investment policy should be as often as you like but on a regular basis. It is most important to review when a life event occurs (marriage, divorce, loss of job) as the event may change your overall plan and strategy.

When you invest your money, I hope that you understand the importance of setting up some sort of process to take before the money is invested. With the help of your financial planner you will go through a process that will develop your investment policy statement (IPS). This IPS will be completed prior to your first dollar being invested.

Although you are putting your trust in your financial planner when it comes to your investment portfolio, it is important to let your planner know your reasons for investing. The main reason may be for retirement, but you may also have an interest in when you can have access to your money and want to make sure your needs are met at the appropriate time.

An investment policy statement can be split into many sections, but I like to use seven specific sections that are built upon each other to meet an agreement between planner and client. The seven sections are goals and priority planning, available and needed assets, target rate of return, limits of risk, investment constraints, asset allocation, and investment selection. As your needs and goals change, your overall statement should be reviewed.

1. Goals and priority planning: Each one of us has unique and different goals that we want to achieve—a high majority of these being accomplished by the use and need of money. This could be buying your first home in the next two years or retiring a few years earlier than originally planned. Once you have your goals in place, it is important to prioritize them to make sure that the amount needed and the timeline attached to each goal is both attainable and realistic. If you have a number of goals that you would like to meet at the same time, then it is important to prioritize and determine which ones can be delayed. If your goals are unrealistic, then you may have to go back to the drawing board to reconsider. Something that is attainable in your mind may be unrealistic from your planner's perspective, so it is important to have an open mind when setting your goals. You may often find that another person's perspective is worth a listen.

2. Available and needed assets: When you start the process of building your investment policy statement, it is important to separate the available assets from the needed assets. Depending on where you are on the retirement timeline, you will most likely be in a shortfall position when you figure out what your needed assets will be to meet each one of your goals. You will need to make some very important decisions in your spending habits to make sure you achieve your goals at your desired timeline. If your timeline becomes an issue, then you may have to downsize your goals or even retire a few years later than initially thought.

3. Target rates of return: This is important both during your working and retirement years. When building financial plans for clients and illustrating the rates of return needed to meet their needs, I always like to 'plan for less and hope for more'. In saying this, I mean that everyone wants a higher return than they are currently receiving, but when the reality of the market sets in, you will be thankful that you planned for less and reviewed your plan on a regular basis, especially if the return is not what you hoped. When discussing target rates of return, it is very important to find out what your risk tolerance is.

4. Limits on risk: This could relate to the type of investments that you put your money into. For example, all investments must be at or below a classification of moderate risk. As the market changes, so too can definitions of risk, so it is important to keep track of this on a regular basis through your regular reviews with your advisor. Risk during your working years could be different than the risk you are willing to take in your retirement years. You could have three different investment goals with each having its own limit on risk and different rates of return. As the market grows, most people don't worry about risk, but as the market corrects downward, they wish that they had kept their limits on risk in check.

You may have to ask around to find someone with an investment policy statement. You don't have to ask specifics. Just start asking general questions which may lead to more specifics later.

5. Investment constraints: When building an investment portfolio, everyone views different types of investments differently. You may want to invest in GICs (Guaranteed Investment Certificates) for the next few years and nothing more. Other investors could limit their investment allocation to half of their money being in stocks (equities) and the other half in bonds (fixed income). If you invest in bonds, you may only want to invest in Government of Canada bonds and not corporate bonds. As more investors are interested in ethical funds and screened funds, you could limit your investment shelf to only certain investment options due to personal preference or other beliefs. As there are always many sources of available investment information in the media, it is important that you communicate your views to your planner on a regular basis.

6. Asset allocation: The mix of cash, bonds, and stocks is one of the most important decisions to make when considering the makeup of your investment portfolio. The definition of what your asset allocation will be should be defined by how long you will need to invest and the risk you are willing to take. One solution could be having more of a conservative investment portfolio *Investment goals often change with transitions in life. From job to career. From renter to home owner. From single to married. Or, other important events that happen in your life.* the closer you are to retirement or until you need a majority of your investments in the future. If you have a higher risk tolerance you may feel comfortable having a higher amount of stocks in your investment portfolio. One important point in deciding on your asset allocation is that if your risk level doesn't meet your funding requirements in the future, you may need to invest more money, lower your standard of living, retire later in life, or lower your retirement income goals rather than agreeing to an asset allocation that would give you sleepless nights.

7. Investment product selection: It is important to be comfortable in the investment products that are chosen to meet your investment goals and retirement objectives. If you want a specific investment that is outside your policy parameters, it is better to go back to section one to clarify your intentions rather than make an exception. One exception may lead to another and then the overall process will not be beneficial to you.

Sharper Focus

- Ask your parents or grandparents if they have an investment policy statement.

- Review your current investment portfolio with your financial planner to see if there should be any changes made or if your investment policy statement needs to be updated.

- If you don't have an investment policy statement you should make an appointment soon with your financial planner to develop one.

CHAPTER 40

Insuring Your Life for Others

*Fun is like life insurance; the older you get,
the more it costs.* - **Kin Hubbard**

Initiating
Conversations

*Do you understand the type of life
insurance you have at work?*

*Is term or permanent life insurance better
for you?*

*Is it important to review the investment
returns in a permanent policy?*

There are Canadians who believe in life insurance and others who don't. Out of those who believe in life insurance, there are those who only believe in term coverage and others that believe in permanent coverage. The goal of a financial planner is to work with his or her client to find out if there is a need for life insurance coverage, the coverage amount that would meet that need and then decide on the type of coverage. Some people have enough assets to not have to worry about meeting their estate planning goals, but the majority of Canadians should consider their needs and goals and then decide if life insurance can fulfill them.

I need to find out how it can work with my personal coverage and what happens with my work coverage when I retire.

Having a conversation about death is not the most enjoyable task, but it is absolutely necessary until you decide if you require coverage or not. If you have a mortgage, you may want coverage to pay it off. If you are single, you may want to leave money to your extended family. If you are married, you may want to make sure all debts (credit and mortgage) are covered plus an agreed upon number of years of salary for the surviving spouse and children. If you are divorced and you are subject to spousal or child support, you may be required to have a certain amount of life insurance coverage until a specified date in the future at which time your obligations have been completed. You may have a charity of which you would like to leave money to. If you are single with no dependants, you may not want coverage and just leave what is left in your estate to your heirs. In most cases, purchasing life insurance is a personal decision, and a financial planner is the perfect person to work with to explore your needs, goals, and other estate planning objectives prior to making a decision to buy or not.

Needs Analysis

When you sit down with your financial planner, a needs analysis should be completed. This needs analysis will explore the 'what if' scenarios based on your family makeup (single, married, dependants, second marriages, widow) as there is not a one size fits all insurance plan.

When considering the amount of life insurance you need, it is important to include as much information as possible, but most importantly the following (list is subject to needs and wants):

Cash requirements at time of death

- Funeral expenses
- Last expenses
- Mortgage outstanding
- Charitable payments
- Salary multiple of deceased (5-8 times salary)
- Education fund
- Taxes owing
- Emergency fund
- Estate settlement costs

Cash available soon after death

- Existing life coverage (personal and group benefits)
- Government death benefits
- Savings

Once you have come to a coverage amount that you are happy with, you will then need to have a discussion with your financial planner about attaching a timeline to different parts of your list. For example, if you have a mortgage that will be paid off in 20 years, then you may decide that term coverage for the mortgage amount is what you would like, as the longer you live the more the mortgage will hopefully be paid down. There are variations of different term coverages that you could apply for depending on the timeline attached to each need.

It all depends on your needs.

If you have estate planning objectives, then permanent insurance may work for you, or you could opt for term coverage that can be converted to permanent insurance (with restrictions) in the future if you are unsure of what your estate planning objectives are at the time of applying for coverage.

Health

When you are applying for personal life insurance, your health status comes into consideration. If your health is not good, then the insurance company may still offer you insurance but at an increased rate. If you smoke, you will pay more when compared to a non-smoker with similar coverage amounts.

When applying for group insurance there will most likely be minimal questions regarding your health for the coverage amount within the plan. The reason for this is that the risk is spread out among all members of the plan and therefore not as many questions are asked compared to personal plans. Small plans may require more health questions. If you want additional coverage within your regular group plan, then additional health questions will likely be applicable as it is an option for group members and not a requirement.

Types of Life Insurance

Term Life Insurance – You will have different terms to choose from. These terms could include 10 year, 20 year, 30 year or coverage to age 100. You can also apply for coverage that renews each year which is called yearly renewable term.

Universal Life Insurance – You will be able to choose the amount of coverage that you would like and combine the coverage with an investment portion that can include equities and fixed income. As long as you continue to pay the required premiums and the rates of return in the investment portion meet your illustrated return objectives, the coverage can last your life time. Depending on the investment portion of the plan, the premiums could be adjusted accordingly. It is important to find out the particulars of this plan with your financial planner prior to buying the coverage or prior to adjusting your premium payments.

Whole Life Insurance – You will be able to choose the amount of coverage that you would like and combine the coverage with an investment portion that usually includes a dividend that you could earn. In the future, this plan could create an opportunity where you will have earned a 'paid up portion' and therefore be able to stop paying your premiums for a lower amount of coverage that would already be paid for. It is important to find out the particulars of this plan with your financial planner prior to buying the coverage or prior to stopping your premium payments.

Investment reviews within your insurance plan are just as important as reviewing your regular investment portfolios.

Even though you may not be able to see the benefits of a life insurance plan, remember that life insurance is not for you but for the family and friends you leave behind.

Sharper Focus

- In your next review meeting with your financial planner be sure to discuss if your financial plan needs life insurance coverage (or additional coverage) depending on what your current needs are today.

- Ask your parents or friends about how they decided on the amount of life insurance they needed when it was time for them to apply. If they don't have life insurance ask them if they can tell you why.

- Review your group benefits plan with your financial planner during your next meeting. See how your group life insurance coverage can work together with any personal insurance coverage you have. Or you may find a need for extra personal coverage.

CHAPTER 41

A $50 Conversation

When you are young and healthy, it never occurs to you that in a single second your whole life could change. - **Annette Funicello**

Initiating
Conversations

Do you wish your benefits coverage at work included critical illness?

Do you know of someone who was able to use critical illness coverage?

If you could only afford one, would you choose life insurance or critical illness?

There is always something more that you want or an additional cost during the month that you didn't expect. When it comes to fitting your financial planning goals into your budget, there is often the conversation of what you *can* see and what you *can't* see (or don't want to see). Being able to calculate a potential market value for your RSP in the future makes it more comfortable to add a RSP contribution to your budget. However, when it comes to planning for the possibility of having a life threatening illness, becoming injured, or dying, it is often more difficult to part with the necessary funds. Not that you don't want to be covered, but that each of us often has the thought that we are indestructible and that something bad will never happen.

More group plans are including critical illness coverage.

I remember having the $50 conversation with Shannon and Marty. After discussing their budget and their concerns of covering their mortgage and other needs with life insurance to meet their estate planning goals, we moved to the asset side of the equation. Shannon was concerned that she and Marty didn't have enough RSP investments at the time for an average early 30s couple saving for their retirement. A valid concern, but I remember asking the question: What is a small RSP contribution going to do for you if something unforeseen happens to your health? It's a topic that nobody wants to discuss (mortality, too for that matter), but it's an important 'what if' conversation you should have with your family and your financial planner. After having a family discussion, it was decided that Shannon would put the $50 monthly contribution to a critical illness policy and wait on increasing her RSP contributions. The decision didn't seem that important at that time, but covering the 'what if' was more important than an extra RSP contribution.

Yes and others could have used it, but the illness did not meet the definition of coverage in their plan.

As our lifespan is increasing, the conversation of morbidity (disability) is as important as mortality (death). Critical illness coverage has its roots dating back to December 3, 1967 in southern Africa. The first human to human heart transplant was performed by a team that included cardiac surgeon Dr. Marius Barnard. He saw a need for those who were diagnosed with a heart attack, stroke, or cancer to have money to cover living costs that would hopefully save the patient from the stress of possibly not being able to work or worse yet lose their home. It was originally called 'dread disease insurance'. In 1995 sales of Critical Illness insurance started in Canada.[1]

Although the original policies mainly covered four main critical conditions (heart attack, stroke, cancer, and coronary bypass surgery), the policies of today can cover over 20 additional conditions. It is important to discuss the likelihood of each condition prior to application. Just as important to understand is the insurer's definition of each type of condition, as they can differ from company to company. As a policy holder you need to know the requirements that the insured has to the insurer once a critical illness is diagnosed by the insured's doctor or specialist. For your reference there is further detailed information on

---

[1] Pg 285 – Chapter 18 Critical Illness Insurance – Disability insurance and other living benefits. Jacqueline E. Figas – CCH 2nd edition. 2009.

types of plans and coverages on the resource page of www.financialfo-tographs.com.

One day a few years after my $50 conversation at Shannon and Marty's kitchen table, I received a phone call from Marty explaining to me that Shannon was diagnosed with breast cancer. Not the news I ever wanted to hear. The great news is that Shannon is now cancer free and had the extra help of the proceeds from her critical illness policy. Here is a list of ways in which her policy helped her and her family:

- Helped transition from two incomes to one
- Paid some medical costs (naturopathic)
- Helped pay for baby sitters when going for treatments or not well
- Help with needs around the house
- Paid for house cleaning
- Enjoyed a great holiday after a very stressful time
- Relieved stress of losing our home
- Relieved stress overall

It depends. Are you single or married? What are your needs going to be if you are diagnosed with a critical illness? Do you have enough savings?

"I guess the big thing for me would be that when you are a young adult with young children and a new mortgage and new in your career, there really could not be a worse time to get cancer. When you are young (not that this is better), you do have your parents to help you out and when you are old your entire home is paid for and your stress is less. As a young adult, you are right in the middle of the most stressful time of your life and adding critical illness makes this time even more difficult.

"Having 1.5 year old twins that depend on you, a husband that had two broken hands, and a new mortgage was stressful enough. Add cancer... not so much fun. If we did not have the money for disability we might have had to sell our home. More stress...on more stress." – Shannon

Sharper Focus

- Talk to a family member who knew someone with a critical illness to see how they were able to adjust their family life with an illness.

- Ask your financial planner to complete a few quotes to find out how much critical illness insurance would cost you.

- Calculate the amount of money you would need to come up with if you were off work due to a critical illness for 3 months, 6 months, or even a year.

CHAPTER 42

Can You Work on Crutches?

My body could stand the crutches but my mind couldn't stand the sideline - **Michael Jordan**

Initiating
Conversations

How many months of income should you have saved in your emergency fund?

Is disability coverage better than life insurance or critical illness coverage?

How does a personal disability plan work with your group benefits plan?

Do you every think about what would happen to your life if you became disabled for a period of time? Most of us don't think about it often but it is important to consider when reviewing your financial plan. A 'what if' scenario doesn't take that much time and it will give you piece of mind if you have the plan in place incase disability does occur. Wouldn't it be nice to have the money necessary to fully recover rather than have to rush back to work? How realistic is that? There are a number of variables that would have to come into play to have enough money to fully recover but if you don't plan then you will wish you had.

As much as possible but plan for 3-5 month's salary.

Do you know how much you are worth to yourself and your family? If you stay healthy until you decide to retire do you know how much money you will make? For example, if you are 30 years old, have an annual salary of $36,000 (no salary increase) and you work until age 65 your potential income that you would have earned is $1.26M. If you are 40 years old, have an annual salary of $120,000 (no salary increase) and you work until age 65 your potential income that you would have earned is $3.0M. These numbers might be hard to comprehend but you have to crunch the numbers in your specific

It all depends on your current situation and future financial planning goals. situation to see what you would have to do to adjust your current lifestyle if a certain amount of your earning power was lost. If you do have a disability and have coverage the insurance company is not going to cover you up to 100% of your current earnings let alone your income until age 65 as there would be no incentive for you to go back to work. Also, there is no guarantee that after you recover that you will be able to return back to work as if nothing happened which will further create a necessity to adjust your lifestyle.

Here are two quotes to show the benefits of having a disability plan:

'It saved my bacon' - Bob. He was able to know that certain costs were covered while he worked hard to get back to health.

'I was glad I had it while I was self-employed' - Jim. He was lucky in that he didn't need to use it but was glad he had coverage as a self-employed business owner.

A great start is to complete a needs analysis to see the amount of money you want to be able to cover during a disability. Then see if you can afford the premium or make the necessary adjustments to your income needs for a more reasonable disability coverage annual premium.

Monthly Needs Analysis

Mortgage or Rent

Property Taxes, house insurance

Home Maintenance

Utilities

Clothing

Food

Credit Card and other debt payments

Auto Expenses

Auto Insurance

Life Insurance

Education expenses and/or savings

Retirement Savings

Other

After you calculate the above monthly expenses how would you pay for the expenses if you are single and could not work for one, two or more months? If you are married and your spouse currently doesn't work how long could you go without work before your spouse had to find a job?

Sources to replace lost income (if you didn't have a personal disability plan)

Group benefits of short term or long term disability coverage - how long will they last?

Savings - how long will this last?

Spouse - how long will this income cover costs?

Loans - difficult if you don't have an income to re-pay in future

I need to find out how it can work with my personal coverage and what happens with my work coverage when I retire.

Equity from your home - last resort

Government benefit plan (CPP) - focus on permanent disabilities that are severe and prolonged

EI -limited coverage

Worker's Compensation - Rules vary across Canada

Investments - tax issues may make this hard to do

Classification

Depending on your profession you are classified into a specific job category for application purposes as each profession may have a few similar tasks but have many different tasks creating different risk categories to the insurer.

Each insurance company that may offer you a disability insurance plan has to take into consideration your job duties and the likelihood that you may become disabled and for how long. Applications for disability insurance are more in depth compared to other insurance coverages.

Depending on what your needs are you can build a plan (subject to limits) that will suit your needs in regards to the premium you are willing to pay or can afford.

In general the more non-guarantees that the insurance company offers you in the future the lower the premium will be. The more guarantees that the insurer offers you the higher the premiums will be. For example; the longer you decide to wait for the benefit to commence the cheaper the premium will be. This is an option if you have other personal or work coverage. The longer the benefit period, the higher the premium will be. In case you don't have extra money saved you can apply for the maximum amount of coverage available.

Sharper

Focus

- Ask your parent's what type of disability coverage they have at work. How does it compare to your plan?

- Ask your financial planner if you can qualify for personal coverage after reviewing your coverage with your employer.

- If you are self employed ask your financial planner to complete a disability needs analysis for you.

CHAPTER 43

Seven

To know how to grow old is the master work of wisdom, and one of the most difficult chapters in the great art of living.
– Henri Frederic Amiel

Initiating Conversations

> *Do you find it difficult to discuss getting older?*
>
> *Do you have family or friends that have made it an important part of their financial plan to make their wishes known if they become dependent on others for assistance in their later years?*
>
> *Do you feel that it is important to be able to live on your own as long as you are able in your retirement years, or would you prefer to move to a seniors' village?*

'Seven' was the name that my great-grandmother gave me. She couldn't say the letter 'K' so 'S' was the next best letter. I don't think she ever did see me, as she was blind for the later years of her life. I remember being in kindergarten and rushing to her 100th birthday after having my tonsils taken out. I guess some of us are lucky being able to remember the most about our 'great' family generation if your parents had you early on in life.

Not so much at 41 as 90 doesn't seem old anymore.

Having longevity on your side is lucky I guess you can say. Being able to see my great-grandmother live to age 107 and my grandparents (mom's side) into their mid-90s was a true blessing. Growing up I remember visiting my great-grandmother at her son's home in Vancouver and then later on at UBC hospital until her passing. I didn't know much of the reasons for the living arrangements, but it was great that she got to live with family as long as possible from my point of view.

I remember having conversations with my grandfather before he passed where he would say that he would "be taken out in a pine box if he

Yes, with power of attorney for both property and health.

had anything to do with it." I don't think this had anything to do with dying, but more with the fact that he wanted to live under his own conditions for as long as possible and maybe had memories about his mother living to age 107 in the hospital.

As I lived fairly close to my grand-parents, I visited many a Sunday for lunch—or shall I say tea, as they believed it to be the main course. Oh the deals I made with my grandparents to make it look like they had eaten their meals so that my uncle wouldn't know. I am sure they knew that I did tell my uncle about their meals, as I wasn't going to let them get away with it. If my grandfather could have lived off Boost® and tea, he would have.

When you have parents that need extra care that you and other family members and friends can't give, decisions need to be made. From my personal experience, I continue to believe that you should be able to try and live as independently as possible in your home. With the amount of home care services available, it is a good option to have as long as it is affordable and the savings are there from investments, pension, or other means. There is another obstacle though, in that your parents may not want to spend the money. Once my grandfather passed it soon became apparent that my grandmother needed ways to increase her social interaction because she was reluctant to even go out to the mall or to spend any money for extra care even though she did talk about the interactions she had with her caregivers. In the end she did sell her home and move to a Seniors Village for the remainder of her life.

Many decisions during your remaining years are often dependent on the available assets and income you have and if you were lucky or smart enough to set the plan in place early on. This is where a product called Long-Term Care Insurance comes into the picture.

I am sure that losing your independence is not the happiest time in one's life. Whether it is progressive or instant, it isn't a thought that you would like to linger on right now as a healthy individual, but it is good to plan—if not for you, for your family.

I think you should be able to live in your home as long as possible. If there is a decline in health or social interaction then maybe a change should be discussed.

Long-term care insurance coverage is one of many conversations that you should have with your family and your financial planner. Goals and available funds are two things that you need to prioritize and calculate in making any decision. If it doesn't make sense today, at least you can be further educated and able to make a well-informed decision in the future if your priorities or available funds change.

Long-term care insurance should not take the place of family involvement, but it is just one solution in the market place that is there to assist when extra funds could be helpful given the many peaks and valleys we have or will experience in the years ahead.

I have included more information on long term care insurance in the resource section at www.financialfotographs.com.

Sharper Focus

- Make time to ask your parents about their wishes as they get older.

- Even if you are a grandchild, a conversation with your grandparents about their wishes can be valuable and a lesson of wisdom learned.

- Make a call to your financial planner to discuss your needs in the area of having money available when you may be in need of long-term care.

CHAPTER 44

Your Home, Your Mortgage

Even the once simple home mortgage now has so many flavors and styles and variations that it is difficult for people to make a decision - **Scott Cook**

Initiating Conversations .

Was your first home purchase and mortgage decision a good experience or a stressful one?

Would you view your personal residence as a future income source or strictly an estate planning asset?

Do you view the risk of a mortgage differently than the risk you take with your investments?

Your principal residence is one of the biggest debts you will ever have and at the same time, the biggest tax free asset the government will give you upon a future sale. The easy part is finding your perfect home. The hard part is making sure you can afford it. Knowing the amount that you can afford for your home purchase is where you should start even before you start looking. You may be able to qualify for more than you realistically can afford so it is important to do some planning beforehand.

Searching for our first home was stressful. Finding the right home for the right price, a location close to parks and multiple offers. Mortgage decision seemed much easier and smoother.

As a home buyer, there is someone that is often forgotten in the overall purchase process and that is a financial planner. You will be looking for a realtor, a mortgage broker and lender, and a lawyer or a notary but don't forget that this purchase will affect your overall financial plan. Your financial planner will add value by making sure that all the financial decisions that are considered will be within your financial reality.

Listed below are six steps that you should consider before your home buying decision is made:

1. Qualify for a mortgage

One of the best decisions you can make before going out to find your dream home is to qualify for a mortgage. Be careful as this does not guarantee that you will receive what you qualify for but it is the closest that you are going to get to knowing where you can begin your house search. The last thing you want to happen is to find your favourite home but not qualify for the necessary mortgage in the end. A good option would be to use a mortgage broker as he or she can save you time and hopefully money as they search the market for lenders on your behalf rather than having to go from lender to lender yourself. The bonus is that the mortgage broker doesn't cost you anything because the re-muneration comes from the lender when you close the deal. Also, your credit is only checked once with the mortgage broker rather than your credit rating being pulled with each personal visit to many lending in-stitutions. The more often you get your credit checked the more it will negatively affect your credit score.

2. Develop a detailed budget

As previously mentioned, even though you may qualify for a mortgage, it doesn't mean that you can afford the specific amount once all your monthly fixed and variable expenses are included in your budget along with your family monthly income. This is important so that you know that your mortgage and other home expenses will be paid every month with current positive cash flow. There will probably be no room for ad-ditional debt so a positive cash flow is a must each and every month. An emergency fund will also need to be created so that funds will be available for those unexpected home expenses. A part of your budget that may need to be trimmed down is your variable spending habits and expenses. This is probably more important in the beginning years of your mortgage due to potential unforeseen issues but is an aspect of your overall financial plan. Having to increase consumer debt because your new budget doesn't work is not a good option at all. If this hap-pens you may be in a position to have to consolidate your debt down the road and it may put you in a position of not being able to afford your home, sell and then be back to square one again.

3. Mortgage Decisions and Down Payment Options

Unless you can pick the winning lottery numbers you are not going to be able to pay off your entire mortgage over the initial term that you choose. An idea that may work for you is to paint a 'debt picture' to see what your situation would look like at the end of different mortgage terms and rates in the future. This would not only include your future mortgage balances but also your future income projections and other purchases that you may need to make in the future. In the past when 0% down payments and amortizations of greater than 25 years were available, the federal government and the lending institutions were trying to make it very accessible for you to qualify for a mortgage. This did not put too much consideration for the future of mortgage holders. We can remember what happened to the mortgage market in the US in 2008 and we were lucky that the same did not happen in Canada.

Our personal residence will be part of our overall estate plan as an asset for our beneficiaries. It will only become an income source if we don't have enough assets to cover our needs later in life.

Mortgage Decisions

Should I choose a fixed rate or a variable rate mortgage?

Mortgage rate decisions should be based on your specific situation, projection of future interest rates and your risk tolerance. When my wife and I bought our first home the market was looking like rates were going to rise and since we really pushed it to put as much as possible as a down payment (savings and RSPs using the home buyers plan) was decided that a fixed rate mortgage was perfect for us. With hindsight it would have been better to have chosen a variable rate but at the time we could not afford to have the mortgage rates go up due to the budget that we created and we decided that this was best for our family. Fixed rates will assist in knowing what your payments will be over the mortgage term that you choose. Variable rates could benefit you but you need an additional plan in place so that you have the ability to lock in a fixed rate in the future if your situation changes or the mortgage market shifts to a position that makes you stressed. Saving as much interest over the life of the mortgage is to your advantage but you need to approach this in a manner that will keep you in your home and build up your tax free equity to benefit your overall financial plan.

Should we choose a shorter term or a longer term mortgage?

When we bought our first home we looked at different rates and terms and ended up deciding on a 10 year term because it met our overall budget and we were still growing in our careers and deciding to start a family. Another important factor in our decision was that even though 10 year terms were not popular at the time (5 year terms seemed to be the norm) the interest rate difference was not that much between a 5, 7 or 10 year term. Therefore, knowing what our payments were going to be for the next 10 years made us happy. Any extra payments we could make from income increases would be going to raising a family and not our mortgage at the time.

When you look at mortgage terms you need to know what the future penalties would be if you choose to re-mortgage in the future. The penalties will be either 3 months interest or something called 'Interest rate differentiation'. Basically the bigger penalty will be the one that you will usually have to pay so it is very important that you request that your lender provide you with possible scenarios and get it written into your contract if possible. The benefit my wife and I had with our 10 year term was that we only had to pay 3 months interest for our penalty when we eventually moved after switching 5 years (and one day) into our term due to the mortgage rules at the time.

How frequently can we afford our mortgage payments?

The sooner you pay down your mortgage the better. Another benefit is you will be saving on interest costs the quicker you pay down your principal. My wife and I started on monthly payments at the beginning because that is what our budget allowed us to do. As our incomes increased we were able to switch to bi-weekly and then for the past couple years we have been paying our mortgage on a weekly basis.

In my view it is better to start with a payment that fits into your budget and then adjust in the future. As long as you are keeping your home emergency fund at an agreed upon level, you can then either switch your payments to bi-weekly or weekly so that you can contribute an extra couple payments each year. Or you can keep the same payment and then contribute extra payments periodically throughout the year or at each anniversary date depending on what your mortgage contract allows.

Be sure to ask your lender to explain all the extra 'bells and whistles' within the contract so that you can compare competing mortgage offers before anything is signed. You have to realize that the lowest mortgage rate may not be the best mortgage for your current situation. It is very important to know how much extra money you can contribute against principal each year (without penalty) so that you can plan accordingly.

Yes, the risk tolerance for our mortgage is lower. We prefer fixed rates rather than variable rates.

What amortization schedule should I choose?

The most common amortization schedule is for 25 years. Along with the term and interest rate the amortization is an important piece of the puzzle that creates your mortgage payment. The longer the amortization period the bigger the mortgage that you can have or the lower the payments will be. When you buy the house you dreamed of your main goal would be to pay down your mortgage quicker and each time your term renews you would try to lower the amortization schedule. The shorter the amortization the higher the payments but your mortgage would be paid off sooner if you keep to the schedule. Just think of the interest that you could save?

Keeping a 25 year amortization and being able to make extra payments throughout the year may be better than committing to a lower amortization in the beginning in case unforeseen negative events were to occur in your life. In my view being able to choose to make extra payments rather than having a required higher payment will benefit your overall plan in case there are other needs elsewhere within your overall financial plan from time to time.

What are my down payment options?

The bigger the down payment the better but you have to be reasonable to make sure you will have enough to cover your moving costs and increases in monthly expenses that you may not be used to.

Home Buyer's Plan (HBP) – The main reason for us being able to max out our down payment was by using our RSPs within the HBP. This is something we had to do even though we would have preferred to only use our savings. Sometimes you have to compromise when a great opportunity presents itself. In my experience the HBP is used very frequently and you just have to set up a RSP plan to pay the borrowed money back on a yearly basis or your required re-payment will be subject to income tax.

Savings and other investments – If you have the benefit of having additional assets to use as a down payment then that would be great. The issues to be thought of before this is decided on are: a) how much tax would be payable when selling a particular asset, b) the loss of possible future gains when your asset is sold and therefore not invested, and c) how much interest would you be saving over the life of the mortgage. With the information from these three issues you will be able to make the decision on whether to use other savings and investments or not.

4. Risk Tolerance

Risk tolerance should not only be considered when making investments. I would argue that your mortgage is also an investment and therefore should be created within your personal and family risk tolerance. From my personal experience I found out very quickly when securing our first mortgage that my investments within the stock market were classified differently when it came to my risk tolerance compared to when we discussed our mortgage options. I am a high risk taker when it comes to my stock market investments but a low risk taker when it comes to my mortgage. Some of the influences in regards to my lower risk tolerance with my mortgage could be because I am married and my wife and I chose to create a family risk tolerance but also I think the risk of not being able to afford my mortgage early on if mortgage rates rose played an important role. Although we have paid more money in interest so far in our mortgage decisions we are happy for it because we don't have to pay attention to interest rates as much.

Whether you are in a variable or fixed rate mortgage make sure that your mortgage broker and lender are there to give you advice in case it could make sense to change your mortgage due to interest rate moves in either direction.

5. Search and find your home

From my experience I have come across clients who call me up when they have found a home they would like to purchase and then ask me what to do next. Even though the above four steps do take time I believe that you will be better off in the end. I know of one situation where the potential home owners made an offer on a home, paid for a home inspection and then went to get qualified for a mortgage where they unfortunately were not able to qualify to purchase the particular home.

With the previous 4 steps completed prior to beginning your search for a new home you will be able to focus on the adventure of finding a home knowing that you have a pretty good idea of the range of prices you can afford and then create your search with this information.

6. Keeping your financial plan and budget up to date.

Once you have purchased your home and moved in it is very important that you meet with your financial planner so that you can update your financial plan and budget with your new mortgage payments and household expenses. Adjust as often as possible and set some goals to pay down your mortgage sooner in the future.

Sharper

- Ask your parent's and grandparent's when and how they became mortgage free.

- If you have a mortgage work with your financial planner on scenario's on how you can pay your mortgage down faster.

- Ask a friend or family member if they believe that paying down your mortgage or contributing to a retirement plan is more important.

CHAPTER 45

The Cap and Gown

*All who have meditated on the art of governing mankind
have been convinced that the fate of empires depends on
the education of youth.* - **Aristotle**

Initiating
Conversations

*If you had the opportunity to go back to school
today, how would you fund your education?*

*What strategy would you use to send your
children to post-secondary school?*

*Do you think your children might value
education more if they borrow or pay for it
themselves?*

The graduation ceremony has just ended and pictures are being taken with you and your son all decked out in his cap and gown. You say to yourself, "What is he going to do in the fall? This is just the start of his future and all we have saved is enough for one year of tuition and books. Beyond that, I don't know where the money is going to come from. What if he doesn't want to go to school? How are we going to save the same amount of money when our daughter graduates in a couple of years?" Then you hear what sounds like a phone ringing, but you wake up to hit the snooze button on your alarm clock. As you emerge from your sleepy fog, you realize where you are going today. You are going to your son's kindergarten graduation.

*Life Long Learning
Plan, equity in my
home or extra
savings as I go
along.*

Not knowing for sure if your child(ren) will attend post-secondary education is a question that each parent has to ask themselves. A parent may want their child to follow in their footsteps or choose a profession as far away from their own as possible.

When I was growing up, I heard my dad say many times that he wanted his kids to be more successful than him. I am sure this is a desire of many

Enough money in an RESP for one year of school and then have it included in our monthly cash flow statement as a fixed expense.

parents. At an early stage in your child's life it is very difficult to determine what your son or daughter may want to do as a career. If he likes to count numbers, does this mean you may have a future financial planner? If she likes to help others, do you have a future teacher in the family? What if your child decides to enter the workforce after high school and doesn't consider post-secondary education at all? It's important to consider the pros and cons of each option you have when investing for your child's future.

What will tuition cost 15 years from now?[1] How much will a home cost in 20 years? What if you decide in the future that your son or daughter is not ready to go out on their own and you would like to hold back some funds to help them once they are ready?

Looking at pictures of my kids since they were born I often wonder what they will become in the future and how my wife and I can add our wisdom to their decisions. Whether they listen or not!

With the Cabbage Patch Kids® craze of the mid 1980s one of my favourite pictures is of my twin sisters, Debbie and Diana, when they were 2 months old. It was a birthday party for my sister Lisa and each of her friends brought their own dolls to join the numerous ones Lisa had. So, my mom took this picture of my twin sisters together with all of the dolls. Fast forward ahead to today and Debbie is a business owner and Diana is a teacher.

---

[1] Visit financialfotographs.com for current numbers.

With increases to education costs each year, it is hard to imagine what the costs will be when your children have graduated from high school. One thing for certain is that the increase will not be following the rate of inflation. If it was only that easy! If the money is there then it will be used. If the money is not there then other options will have to be considered.

My wife and I have decided that we would like to have enough money saved up so that our children will be able to cover the first year of college or university without having to work. Not that they wouldn't be able to work, but because I know I couldn't handle school and working at the same time. On the other hand, my wife accomplished it perfectly. The reason for one year of school is so that they can say that they tried it whether they carried on with it or not. I just know how easy it is to wonder, "What if I had gone to school?" Also, at this point, I don't know what they are going to do and paying off our mortgage and then turning our mortgage payment into an education expense or other expense for our children is the way I want to go. Things can change.

When talking with your financial planner, it is important to discuss all options when saving for your children's future. I have always said that I would never buy into a government program just for the incentive the government has given, but that is only my viewpoint. Four options that you could have are a Registered Education Savings Plan (RESP), Tax Free Savings Account (TFSA), In-Trust Account (ITF), and regular non-registered investments or savings. There is not one correct answer, but reviewing the options and tax issues prior to investing is an important first step.

RESP – If the government gave me a grant to invest in future education, it would appear to be a great deal. You could argue either way. From a financial planning perspective, I would argue that you would need to ask yourself the following question: "What is best for my family today and into the future" For example if you invest $1000 into your RSP or put $1000 against your mortgage, is it better than contributing $1000 to an RESP for your child(ren)? The general answer is that *it depends*. *It depends* on your marginal tax rate to see how much of a tax refund you receive from your RSP contribution. *It depends* on the amount of interest you will save over the life of your mortgage for the contribution against principal of your outstanding mortgage. *It depends* on if you would be able to pay for the school costs when your child(ren) go to school if you don't have a mortgage and your RSP contributions and values are where you want them to be.

RESPs have rules that need to be followed regarding contributions, grants that are received, withdrawals, if you have other children within the plan if one child doesn't go to school, and if you want to close down the account. Just make sure each dollar that you contribute within your financial plan will be the right thing to do at that time for you and your family, today and into the future.

Having your child(ren) pay for their own post-secondary education could be better in the end. It all depends on the individual.

TFSA – This is a great plan for Canadians to use for many reasons. You can use this for your own investing needs, savings for emergencies, and even a savings vehicle for the needs of your children, today and in the future. Any investments are tax sheltered like an RRSP or RRIF so that you don't have to worry about taxes while the investments are within the plan, and the extra bonus is that when you cash the funds out, any capital gains that you have are tax free. You have to remember that you don't receive any government tax break (like an RSP) because investments are made with after tax dollars. PLEASE NOTE: If you are investing in a TFSA, be careful that you know the contribution and withdrawal rules as over-contributions are subject to penalties.

ITF – This example of an in-trust account is an 'informal trust'. This plan is great for saving for your child(ren)'s future education needs, a down payment for a home, or for needs while still defined as a minor. The investments that you would include in an ITF account are managed on the behalf of the beneficiary until they reach the age of majority. Any contributions made to the ITF account can't be returned to the contributor and all proceeds must be only used for the beneficiary. Make sure you talk with your financial planner prior to opening up an ITF account to make sure all the attribution rules, taxation rules and investment options are known prior to any money being invested. If you invest money and your child turns the age of majority he or she may end up spending the money on something different than you had planned.

Non-registered – If you want full control of all investments so that you can make changes to how you distribute the assets, then a non-registered account may be a good alternative to an ITF account (as long as you have maxed out your TFSA contribution limit). You do get full control of the assets, but you have to pay all taxes received from your portfolio. Make sure you speak to your financial planner about non-registered tax deferral programs that might be available if you decide to diversify your portfolio in the future. This way you can choose when to pay the taxes on any gains or defer to a later date when you may be at a lower tax bracket. Remember, when you invest in a non-registered plan, it is the after tax return you are looking for. If you sell, pay the tax on capital gains then re-invest in another investment you need to calculate how long it will take to make up for the tax you paid.

Sharper

Focus

- If you have children, put a plan in place that meets your budget to save for your children's future.

- Ask your spouse how he or she paid for their education. Was any money used for other needs if school was not attended?

- Ask your parents or grandparents on the reason why they did or did not save money for your education or other needs.

CHAPTER 46

What if the Numbers Don't Match?

A goal without a plan is just a wish

– Antoine de Sain-Exupery (1900-1944)

Initiating
Conversations

Did your parents have a plan when you were growing up?

When should you start planning for retirement?

What changes would you be willing to make if you wanted to retire without the required assets?

Imagine this: you and your spouse are two months from signing your retirement papers, as you have decided to retire early together. You have both spent the weekend crunching numbers and have completed your very first monthly retirement budget by adding up all your income sources during retirement and itemizing your expenses. The numbers just don't match.

You will have the *time* to enjoy the things you have always wanted to do but can you *afford* it? You both want to travel, play a round of golf each week, and spend more time with your grandchildren. Retirement is supposed to be easy, isn't it?

My parents didn't have the time early on in their marriage as they lived paycheque to paycheque.

In the little amount of time you have spent discussing your retirement, you both agree that some financial planning work must be done in order to ensure a retirement with no cash flow concerns. You wonder what options you have to create a positive monthly cash flow during retirement and what will happen if you can't meet this goal.

You want to make sure that time is on your side once you have both decided to retire. What could your retirement picture look like if you plan for retirement sooner than later? You now understand what your parents have been telling you for the past five years: *"Time is of value when it comes to retirement planning."* The more time you can spend planning, the more options you may have at your disposal. It is better to know that the numbers will not match now than after you work your last day. Adjustments can always be made during your working years, as creating your desired retirement standard of living and living it rather than having to continuously adjust it during retirement should be an important goal for both of you.

Retirement plans can always be updated during your working years. Therefore, start early so you can work towards meeting your retirement goals one step at a time.

It would be great to control the amount of healthy retirement years you will have, but we all know this is not possible. We have to take what we are given. It's of some comfort that you know that people are living longer these days, but on the other hand it scares you because you don't want to go broke if money is not smartly saved prior to retirement.

Starting the retirement conversation with your financial planner early on in your working years can only benefit you so that planning is done right and not rushed. When you sit down with your financial planner, he or she may ask you to consider your perfect retirement number and then plan accordingly to make sure the target is met. If you fail to plan and your perfect retirement number is not met, there are six options that you will need to consider:

Option 1 – Increase the amount you are able to keep invested during your retirement. This option may not be ideal. You are going to need to find a way to decrease your planned spending habits (increase monthly positive cash flow) to leave additional money to be invested. Although you may find some room in your fixed expenses, the area that you will need to revise is your variable expenses (e.g. golf games). One idea that may work is to put all annual pension increases—confirmed or planned—into savings rather than increase monthly spending. But, inflation will have something to say about that!

Option 2 – Increase the risk in your investment portfolio(s). You hope this will increase the rate of return you will receive throughout retirement to make up for any monthly shortfalls. Depending on your timeline, this option may or may not be a good one. In retirement you should be in the process of decreasing, not increasing, your risk tolerance. A downside of increasing your risk tolerance and hoping for a higher return is if the market goes through a correction at the wrong time (when you need the money) and your portfolio loses money. The result would be that you would have to decrease your standard of living during retirement so that you hopefully don't outlive your money.

Option 3 – Continue to work part-time during retirement so that you can continue to receive a regular income and delay the need to start drawing from other retirement sources (e.g. RSP) or at least decrease the amount you need to withdraw. It may be to your benefit to continue to work past your desired retirement age depending on whether you have a pension plan and the type of plan it is.

Option 4 – Decrease your desired standard of living during retirement. You normally don't need 100% of your working income during retirement due to having fewer expenses (e.g. no mortgage and no kids living at home). It is important to not deplete all your savings during the early years of retirement and rely on government plans for the remaining years of your life.

Option 5 - Adjust your estate plan. If you would like to leave money to family or a charity as part of your estate plan, then knowing you have enough left over is another need to consider when crunching your retirement numbers. You may have a specific asset value that you want to leave or it may be just *'whatever the house is worth'* at the end. You have to remember that the value of your house may become your only asset to fund long term care or assisted living if your health is not your friend towards the end of your life. You also have to plan for one spouse to outlive the other and crunch those numbers too.

I may have to work part-time to give me some variety in retirement and not deplete my assets so quickly.

Option 6 – Downsize so that you can utilize the equity out of certain assets such as your home. This would add to the funding of your retirement cash flow needs. It's not the ideal situation, but you may find that you want to downsize anyway. By doing so, you may create enough investment equity in your portfolio to make up for any shortfalls that you have.

All of the six options may not put a smile on your face; however, these are necessary discussions to have so that you can create an effective retirement plan that makes you happy. You worked hard for what you have! Setting your retirement goals as early as possible and planning the required cash flow to fund them is very important while keeping your investment risk tolerance at a comfortable level.

Sharper  Focus

- If your parents are retired ask them if they retired when they wanted to.
- If so, how often did they change their retirement plan during their working years?
- If not, did they have to change their retirement spending habits?
- If you will have pension income during retirement make an appointment with your financial planner to see how the pension income will compliment your current financial plan.
- Make time in the next month to write down everything you plan to do during retirement. Find out what the costs would be today (if you were to retire) and then work with your financial planner to find out the costs (add appropriate inflation) in the future during your hopeful retirement years.

CHAPTER 47

What do I do with my pension plan?

Retirement at sixty-five is ridiculous.
When I was sixty-five I still had pimples.

- George Burns (1896-1996)

Initiating
Conversations

Do you feel that your pension plan is a part of your overall retirement plan, or separate from it?

Do you find your pension plan statement confusing?

If you have a spouse, do only one of you have a pension? If so, how has that influenced your current financial plan?

Do I have enough invested for my retirement? I don't know the answer unless I know what 'enough' means to you. Often people base their retirement value on their RSP statements and other investments they have. They often miss one piece of their future retirement nest egg, their retirement plan at work. Not on purpose but because they often don't understand what it means. Sure they get statements each year but it is often filed away or still in the unopened envelope. Not a good habit to have especially when these updates are important information.

It should be part of my overall plan but I often don't have time to focus on finding out how everything works together.

The government and big corporations tend to have a defined benefit pension plan (DBPP) and others could have a defined contribution pension plan (DCPP). To cut down costs and future liabilities companies are often preferring to not have a regular pension plan but rather a group RSP (with employer matching benefits), a deferred profit sharing plan (DPSP) or other savings plan as a benefit to their employees. Good-bye to the golden handshake as it was known in the past.

I often find that many people are not able to explain their work retirement plans to me which is always a concern of mine. The concern is that employees are not getting educated about their plan through their employer. Therefore, I find it very important to gather the necessary information so that my client and I can put all their investment, retirement, and savings information together to create a complete investment analysis within their financial plan. Having updated information from work retirement plans on a regular basis will assist your financial planner in making the necessary adjustments to your current financial plan. You will see below that the employee will have more work to do with a defined contribution plan than a defined benefit plan.

Defined Benefit Plan – This is the type of plan that you and your employer contribute to and your benefit during retirement is based on the contributions, your years of service and your age. When you review your plan it is important that you understand the projection of the earliest retirement date with a reduced pension, earliest retirement date with an unreduced pension, your bridge benefit and retirement benefit after the normal retirement age. It is also very important to find out if there will be an inflation increase during retirement.

Defined Contribution Plan – You and your employer contribute to this plan but your benefit is based on the choices that you make within the investment options throughout the life of the plan. Risk and reward are two very important concepts to consider when making the investment choices. Hopefully your employer will have the administrator of the plan as a resource for your investment choices and to answer any questions you may have. But it's a good idea if you can ask your financial planner for assistance (of which disclosures will need to be signed).

If you have a GRSP, DPSP or other savings plan as part of your work retirement plan instead of a traditional pension plan it is just as important to receive regular updates as the investment choices are often up to you with no recommendations allowed from your employer. With an ever changing stock and bond market it is important that you keep track of your investment progress just like you would with your personal RSP.

It gives me numbers but I need to know how the information relates to my overall financial plan.

If you change jobs prior to your official retirement, you need to explore the options that you will receive in regards to your vested pension amount. The term 'vested' means the value that is yours and does not have to be given back to your employer. These options include transferring your pension value to a new plan, transferring to your new employer's pension plan or leave it with your former employer. It's always best to get all the necessary information to compare rather than making a quick decision that you can't change in the future.

Deferred Pension – this option would show you what you are entitled to as a pension during retirement if you leave your 'vested' pension amount with your former employer. There could be a chance to change your mind in the future so it is critical that you find out when your final decision date is. Leaving your pension amount with your former employer could include a benefit plan (i.e. medical and dental) during your retirement so you should double check this possibility. Another important question to ask is if the pension amount will or could be adjusted for inflation. Also, the future health of the pension plan is a very important issue but is one that most times you will have to go with a 'gut' feeling. I would recommend that you find out as much information as possible so that you can make the most informed decision.

Commuted Value – this is the lump sum available in today's dollars of your future pension benefit that has vested with you. It could be a combination of an amount that can be transferred and tax deferred within a personal registered plan (i.e. RSP) or locked-in registered plan (i.e. LIRA). This amount could also include money that is above the allowed amount that you could transfer to a tax deferred account (excess of the income tax limit) and therefore is taken as cash. You need to find out what the deadline is for a decision to be made as the value will only be guaranteed for a limited period of time. If the deadline is missed you need to request another commuted value calculation which could vary from before. You also need to know the final date a commuted value amount can be taken.

Before you make the decision on what to do with your pension options it is always smart to get your financial planner involved so that he or she can hypothetically compare your deferred pension amount to what your commuted value could look like in the future if you take the commuted value and invest it personally until your retirement date. Not a perfect comparison but when you take an investment in your own hands you should know that the value becomes what you have to live with which could make you better off or not compared to a future deferred pension.

Your decision could also involve what you plan to do within your existing financial plan and if you have any specific monetary goals within your estate plan. It is always good to look at the big picture when making these decisions as well as a few 'what if' scenarios. You worked hard to earn your pension so make sure you get the most value out of it as possible in the end.

Old Age Security (OAS) and Canadian Pension Plan (CPP) are two other pension plans that need to be included in your retirement projections. Although the amount that you will actually receive can change in the future you always want to include an approximate amount and adjust it each time you update your retirement projections. OAS is funded by the federal government out of tax revenues and CPP is basically a 'pay as you go system' paid to retirees by the income earners of the day. If the funding resources of these plans don't meet the need to pay out the pension balances then we would see changes in the amounts that an employee and employer contribute to the CPP and the government could raise taxes to increase the OAS outstanding balances.

> *We have different risk tolerances within our overall retirement planning projections.*

If you have reached retirement age and have received your pension options it is important to consider all options that you have. You could have 6-8 choices of different pension amounts that match with different guaranteed terms. It is important to go over your pension options with your financial planner so that different scenarios can be put together to better illustrate how your different pension options will work together with your financial plan and your estate plan.

Sharper Focus

- Contact your local federal taxation office to find your history of CPP contributions and projected CPP income at retirement.

- If you have a pension, make sure that your financial planner receives your annual statements.

- If only one spouse has a pension plan, how does this affect the investment strategy of the other spouse? Review this with your financial planner.

CHAPTER 48

What can I do with my RRSP?

I think you've got to take your time and make sure you're making choices that are smart for you.
— **Matthew Fox**

Initiating
Conversations

Is variable or fixed income more important to you?

What can you do if you think you are going to outlive your money?

What needs to be done before you can decide to retire?

You have just retired and would like to know what your options are with your RRSP accounts. Also, you want to know how much income you could expect and what possible guarantees there may be for you and your spouse. You do like the option of flexibility for estate planning purposes so you would like to gather information before you make an educated decision.

A combination of variable and fixed income would be a good mix for me.

Longevity has a big part in this decision for you. With more people living longer the worry of outliving your money is of concern for many. Flexibility is another big part for those who want more control over their investments and have estate planning objectives that they would like to be carried out once they have passed.

As a RRSP account holder you have three options upon the maturity age at the time of your decision. The three options are cashing it out, changing the registration to a RRIF or buying an annuity. Or, any combination of the three.

Option One:

Cashing out your account(s). This choice usually doesn't have much popularity due to the tax implications of adding the whole balance of the redemption to your income within the tax year of the RRSP withdrawal. When you contributed to your RRSP throughout your working years you will most likely want to get the most out of your contributions which cashing out would not be a good solution. This would potentially work for very small RRSP accounts but you need to figure out the tax implications before any choice is made.

Option Two:

Transferring your account(s) to a Registered Retirement Income Fund (RRIF). This is a popular choice among Canadians as this gives you the most control over your money. The holdings can be similar to your RRSP account but it is always good to review your portfolio holdings and risk tolerance at the time of transferring from a RRSP to a RRIF account as your goals and risk tolerance could have changed.

The main difference is that you will now have to withdraw the minimum amount from your investment holdings. You can withdrawal more but there is a minimum amount each year. The applicable withdrawal amounts can be found on the *Financial Fotographs* website under *resources* for reference. Whether the withdrawal amount is the minimum or another amount you can set up the withdrawals to be on a monthly, quarterly or annual basis with most financial institutions.

Option Three:

Transferring your account(s) to an Annuity. This is a choice that you have but it is not as popular. This has a lot to do with the interest rate environment at the time of purchase and due to the fact that transfers to a RRIF are more popular for income flexibility reasons.

Choosing an annuity is much more than just deciding on the annual amount that you will

Work with your financial planner to create a number of scenarios so that you are comfortable with the income decision you make.

Calculate the amount of money you need to live on during retirement. Then compare it to your current assets and future projections.

receive. The decision should be made after reviewing your overall retirement plan with your financial planner.

Annuities give you peace of mind that you will be receiving a regular income but also have some possible negative aspects you should understand before making your decision. You will lose control over your investment and income options since your income will be agreed upon with your annuity provider within the contract. Interest rates are a major factor in annuity rate calculations when you are searching for a particular income amount.

If you are not a risk taker and believe that you may outlive your money then an annuity could be an option for some or all of your investments. If you want an income for your surviving spouse then an annuity could be an option.

It is important for you to explore your RRSP options with your financial planner. You need to make the correct decision that you feel most comfortable with to meet your retirement needs as well as your estate planning needs. Once you include your CPP, OAS and other pension amounts into your retirement needs calculation, you will find out the shortfall that you may have in which your RSP accounts will assist in fulfilling your needs. You could always transfer your money into a RRIF and each year review with your financial planner the option of transferring a portion to an Annuity at that time. Having different income sources can assist you in diversifying your retirement income but you need to feel comfortable with your decision. Future decisions will be based on the current interest rate environment, how your investments have performed, your changing retirement income needs and your estate plan at that time. As long as you keep all your options open and work with a financial planner that will keep you up to date on your retirement plan then that will give you the tools to make the best decision for you and your family.

Sharper Focus

- Calculate all your retirement sources of income and compare the total with your anticipated retirement income needs to see if there is a shortfall or surplus.

- If you are close to retirement ask your financial planner to put together illustrations to show you examples of potential income flows from both RRIF accounts and annuities.

- If your parent's are retired ask them what helps them make their decisions when it comes to retirement income options that they can control.

CHAPTER 49

The Retirement Years: How Much Do I Need?

I need to retire from retirement. - **Sandra Day O'Connor**

Initiating Conversations

> *Do you see yourself retiring in your mid 60's?*
>
> *Will you have a different plan for your active years compared to your older retirement years?*
>
> *Do you see yourself having to care for your parents in their older years which may alter your financial plan?*

As more and more people live longer than generations before, there is the possibility of being retired for more years than the number of years you worked. Therefore, I am finding more people wanting to 're-tire from retirement' to some extent. I don't mean that you will want to go back to work full-time, but you may find yourself at a 'wits end' during retire-ment because of boredom. After the 'retirement honeymoon' is over you may find yourself searching for ideas to fill your day.

Semi – retiring as long as I am still effective in what I do and still enjoy it.

During retirement you will find that you will have the *active* years and the *local* years which are mainly dependant on your desires, assets and health. The active years are going to be the time when your health is at its best and that you are able to fulfill your retirement goals of travelling and other activities that you think may not be possible if you experience health issues. The *local* years are dependent on your desire to stay close to home due to money, family and health issues.

As with the working years you need to ask your financial planner 'how much do I need?' And again the answer should be 'it depends'. Without knowing what you want to do, what your budget is and what your estate planning needs are it is hard to answer the question. What

I will hope to accomplish most of my 'bucket list' while I am still able. do you want to do? This question could be answered many ways. But most of the answers will center on how much money you have. Not every activity costs money but the majority do.

To answer the question: 'How much do I need?' Here are some questions to consider:

What income can you rely on? Outside of government benefits (i.e. CPP and OAS) do you have a company pension or a RRIF portfolio to draw income from?

Do you have a mortgage? A great goal to have during retirement is to be mortgage free? Due to a decrease in your income during retirement it is nice not to have that mortgage payment. If you do still have a mortgage you need to decide if you are in a position to be able to keep it or if you need to downsize. This could be a decision that needs to be made depending on what your retirement goals are and what your estate planning goals are.

How long are you going to live? How long are you going to be healthy? Two questions which are not easy to answer but do effect your retirement plans. You will always have the dilemma of wanting to enjoy a retirement you worked hard for and not wanting to outlive your money if you spend too much too early. You can look at your family tree to see how long your previous generations lived.

What are your estate planning goals? You should always review your will throughout your life on a regular basis to make sure your desires are always up to date. Once you decide that you are contemplating retirement it is imperative that you review your will and update your estate plan for two reasons. Firstly, to make sure that your legacy is defined while you are still able to make the decisions and if you are not able to, who you want to make your voice heard. Secondly, depending on what your estate plan is you need to know how much money will be needed to facilitate your legacy plans which will affect your retirement plan. If you require a certain amount of money left or if you have a life insurance plan to meet your needs then you should discuss this with your financial planner. Or if your answer to 'how much you want to leave' is 'whatever is left' then this is important to discuss too.

Are the kids still at home or may they be coming back to live? With more people finishing off their careers first and then having children later in life do you plan on having post secondary tuition costs close to your retirement or during the early years of retirement? Or due to circumstances do you see your children moving back home for a period of time? The closer you are to retirement the more specific you can be. The further away from retirement you are the more money you may need to put aside to use if necessary or to add to your retirement nest egg if not needed.

What is your bucket list? Ever since the 2007 movie starring Morgan Freeman and Jack Nicholson came out everyone seems to have a 'bucket list'. If something on your bucket list will cost money then it has to be added to your retirement plan. My bucket list will include travelling to England to see some 'football' games (wearing the correct jersey) and an American football game, baseball game and hockey game on the East Coast of the US by watching the Patriots, Red Sox and Bruins respectively. I'll start saving today.

Will you be caring for your parents? With family members living longer these days this possibility is more relevant today than generations before. If your parent's don't have the resources (if they do tell you) then you can plan accordingly. What I suggest is to have a family meeting with your parents and siblings to discuss this issue. Not a conversation that everyone would like to have but it is necessary. Don't be afraid to bring this question up with your parent's as you are only there to help and not to hinder.

These questions are sometimes not easy to answer depending on your stage of life. Regardless it is important to have these discussions with your financial planner so that a reasonable retirement can be created and built upon in the years going forward. If you wait too late then changes that could have been done during your 'working years' may not be able to be made in time. Plan smart because you deserve to reap the rewards of your hard

Yes, as part of a family decision.

work prior to your decision to retire. Hopefully you will have planned enough so that you won't have to retire from retirement because you haven't planned.

Sharper  Focus

- Set up a meeting with your financial planner to crunch your financial and retirement numbers.

- Try to set up a family meeting with your parents and siblings. Or at least try and have a conversation with your parents centered on what they would like to happen if their health started to fail or they choose to downsize because they find activities difficult.

- Make up your 'bucket list' and put a price tag beside each entry.

CHAPTER 50

The Working Years:
How Much Do I Need?

If you have a garden and a library, you have everything you need. - **Marcus Tullius Cicero**

Initiating
Conversations

What is the difference between what you need and what you want?

If you win the lottery would that be enough to survive on?

Have you changed your needs and wants over the years?

Wouldn't it be nice if a garden and a library were everything that we would need! But, we all know that is far from the truth. Each of us has a unique definition for how much is needed in order to meet our personal needs of today while hoping that our needs of tomorrow are taken care of. As the years go by and life events happen, that definition will need to be re-defined. Difficult choices will need to be made and a big part of your definition will be created from your ability to prioritize what is important to you.

You need to take a piece of paper and draw a line down the middle then write your needs on the left side and your wants on the right.

But we can always dream! A financial planner could receive an email similar to this one from a client:

Dear My Financial Planner:

I would like to know how much I need to be able to live comfortably from today until retirement. And, at the same time, I need to know how much I will need to save in my retirement plan to live a comfortable retirement with no worries at all. I know that I can't tolerate any stress as life will be stressful enough. I am sure that this is an easy number to determine and that you have the right calculator to be able to tell me the magic number.

It depends on what your needs and wants are in the end.

Sincerely,
Your always realistic client.

That would be the ultimate answer to get from your financial planner—one specific 'magic' number that would meet both your working years needs and your retirement financial goals!   You would not need a financial planner at all. Just a calculator.

I have the answer to this question. The answer is 'it depends'. It's not the easy way out. It is the financial truth. The mathematical question depends on a number of variables. Some variables you have more control over than others. In reality you would not like the magic number you were given because it would probably be too high. Also, your financial planner wouldn't be able to define your specific number as you would need to answer a number of questions. Then you would hope that everything else that you can't control will work in your favour until you declare your intention to retire many years down the road.

Questions you have the most control over:

How much money are you going to earn? With experience and education, you have a better chance to choose which job you take. This will assist in defining a realistic standard of living. You will need to review your standard of living as circumstances change throughout your life.

How long do you want to work? This may be dependent on your health in the end, but hopefully the question is answered once you figure out the money you will need to meet your standard of living needs and wants in retirement. You have to remember to put a plan in place to meet your needs and wants during your pre-retirement years which will affect the money that will be available during retirement.

What will be a comfortable mortgage payment? The purchase of your home will most likely be the biggest debt you will have during your lifetime. You will need to decide on a mortgage payment you can handle (while taking into consideration future payment changes due to a change in mortgage rates) and then shop for your home from there. The mortgage you qualify for is not always the mortgage you can afford.

What is going to be included in your budget? A budget includes both fixed and variable costs. The fixed costs (food, shelter, clothing, heating, etc.) can't be missed, so your variable costs (eating out, cable, transportation, etc.) need to be prioritized on a monthly basis at least. When fixed costs go up, variable costs need to come down, unless your income increases at the same time.

How much investment risk are you willing to take? Risk is a hard word to define as it means different things to different people. Investors tend not to worry about risk when the market is going up; however, they do think they have too much risk when the market falls. If you know what your *They are much different from when I was single to now that I am married with kids.* standard of living is going to be during your working years and you are happy with your retirement projections then a risk level can be defined. If it makes you uncomfortable, then you have to re-examine your standard of living by maybe spending less or deciding to defer your ideal retirement age so that you can take less risk to meet your retirement portfolio objectives.

Questions you have less control over:

What will inflation be? – We all know that prices go up—sometimes higher than we want them to! There are many variables that create inflation, and your budget and standard of living have to be altered accordingly. The supply and demand game seems to never end.

What income changes will you experience? – You can't control how the economy is going to behave during your lifetime. Therefore, you need to be ready for unexpected changes at your job. You may decide to take another job opportunity that pays less or your job may become obsolete. Worse yet, your boss could tell you that he is closing the company down at the end of the month.

What will the market returns be? – You can control within reason the investment risk that you take in your portfolio, but you can't control market returns. With the help of a financial planner you can create an investment portfolio where you can be as pro-active as possible to changes in the market so that necessary reactions to market volatility will be minimal. Communication is a must with your financial planner.

How long will you live during retirement? With the advancement of science, we all one day may be able to take a test to tell us how long we will live. The more reasonable concern may be whether or not you are going to outlive your money. Outside of a private pension or government benefits, it is important to hypothesize as to whether or not you will outlive your money. If you don't outlive your money then there will be more for your heirs. If you start to outlive your money where will the money come from to make up the shortfall? This is why it is good to plan early so that the necessary changes can be made.

'It depends' is not the answer you would look for if you ask your financial planner, "how much do I need?", but it is the right answer to start. Unless you answer the questions above and maybe a few more that are important to you, the amount of money you think you need and what you end up needing can be two very different numbers.

Sharper Focus

- Have a goal this week to create a budget that includes your monthly take home income and the monthly expenses you have.

- Contact your financial planner to have a review meeting to make sure your current plan meets your current needs. Also, ask for a projection of what your current investment portfolio could be at your desired retirement age.

- Review your budget this month to see if there should be any changes made in the coming months.

CHAPTER 51

Planting A Tree

He plants trees to benefit another generation.

- Caecilius Statius

Initiating
Conversations

What is an example of how a friend or family member left a legacy?

During retirement what do you want to leave as a legacy with your time?

What is one gift that you have that you want to teach others while you still can?

I remember travelling to the local tree nursery with my class when I was 5 or 6 and as we left we each received a small seedling. This small seedling was planted in my parent's backyard and as I grew up, I was excited to see it grow. It's amazing how something so small can grow so big. Although that small seedling won't grow a forest it will leave a lasting impression on my parent's backyard and maybe be the home to a bird nest one day.

Being a friend. Showing interest in what I do.

As you live your life I am sure that you have thought about the positive impact that you can have in your children's lives, the community in which you live and the world as a whole. In our 'working years' it is often hard to find enough time in the day to get done what we want to get done. It is often in our 'retirement years' where we will find ourselves looking at ways to keep ourselves busy. It's not always with money that we can make a difference but with our time.

It wasn't until I became a father that it really hit me as to what type of legacy I would want to leave for my family and others. I know I will most likely have more time when my kids are older and retirement hits, but I have always believed that it was important to give back to others through-

Being able to spend time where needed. Pass wisdom along to others if asked. Be able to leave an education fund for any future grandchildren.

out our entire lives. One way I feel I give back is through my profession as a financial planner. Teaching others about financial planning and being involved in promoting financial planning to others throughout Canada has been a goal of mine. I had the privilege of speaking to grade 11 and 12 students at a local high school of which I mentioned earlier on in this book. Before my children came along, I was able to help out and lead a children's program within the community for a few years. Now that my children are young, I find it important to make family time and create a work schedule in which I don't miss family time. We all live busy lives, but it is often through reflection when a family member or friend passes away when you ask yourself if you could have spent more time with that person.

Putting together your will and discussing your estate plan is not the easiest conversation for most of us. Myself included! But without your wishes completed in writing others may not know what you wanted to do with what you left behind.

Talking about leaving a legacy should not be forgotten because you may think it is all about your ego. It's not about ego, rather what is important to you and putting the plans in place to facilitate your wishes.

Adding your legacy wishes to your financial plan whether you are 19 or 99 is important as your plans can always be changed. If you don't have your 'legacy' discussion with your family then you may never get to it.

Creating a place where society doesn't rely on debt and to assist others in building a standard of living that they deserve.

Why should your financial planner be in your legacy conversation? Your financial plan can be affected by your legacy goals. Depending on what your plans are, it could affect your standard of living during your working years or retirement years. Many goals that you may have will involve money. It could be an education plan for your children or grandchildren. It could be leaving an amount of money to your favourite charity or cause that is important to you. There are solutions available that will help you be able to experience the outcome of these goals while you are living or once you have passed on. It just starts with a conversation and then a plan can be set in place. What is or could be your tree within your financial plan today or in the future?

Sharper

Focus

- Put thoughts to paper in establishing what your legacy will be and share it with a friend or family member.

- If your legacy plan includes a need for assets, then book a time to discuss your list with your financial planner.

- When you pass away what is a sentence that someone could use to describe you?

CHAPTER 52

Should I Plan If I Am Single?

I love being single. It's almost like being rich. – **Sue Grafton**

Initiating
Conversations

Do you need a budget if you are single?

Is life insurance important to you if you are single with no dependants?

Is having a will important if you are single with no dependants?

Everyone has a unique financial plan and being single is no different. Everyone has different goals and objectives when writing a financial plan depending on their family dynamics, the amount of money they have, and the lifestyle that they want. So I asked Lisa, Wendy, and Diane to give me insight from their individual perspectives on aspects of a financial plan as a single Canadian without any dependants.

Financial Plan

I believe that everyone should have a financial plan, even if everything that is included is only on a single piece of paper. It is a start at least.

Essential to a stress-free life.
- Lisa

"I think it is very important to have financial goals—both big and small—for your life. Long range ideas about how you want to live and when you want to retire, or even shorter-term goals, like where you want to go for your vacation, are very important. The short term goals are usually just a matter of saving money, but the long term goals require the expertise and assistance of a financial planner. And because a financial planner has a larger picture and is more objective about your money and life goals, they are in a better position to assess whether those goals are realistic or not and can help you adjust goals and plans accordingly." – Lisa

"A financial plan and goal for early retirement is of primary importance for me." - Diane

Budget

Effective spending and saving doesn't happen as often if you don't learn how to keep track. Even if you are living paycheque to paycheque, you should still keep track of your monthly income and expenses so that you can ensure you are spending and saving as efficiently as possible. Spending wisely and saving smartly are difficult to do if you don't learn how to keep track of your cash flow.

> "I'm convinced budgeting is essential to a stress-free life. It needn't be a very rigid, detailed affair. If you can keep in mind a goal you feel strongly about, then making small daily sacrifices (cutting back on restaurant meals or entertainment) is easier to bear. Not indulging in those little extravagances could feel like deprivation, but if you keep in mind that the money is going towards those larger goals, and over time you can see it begin to accumulate, then these budget decisions will leave you feeling a sense of self control, self-satisfaction, and self-efficacy, rather than a feeling of want and lack." - Lisa

> "Personally, I'm lousy at budgets or spending plans—the money comes in and it all has somewhere to go! Then something happens in life which causes a re-direction of certain funds." - Wendy

Buying a Home

Hopefully buying a home is a goal for every Canadian. The reality is that for many reasons, this doesn't happen when you want it to. After the rent and all the bills are paid, there often isn't much money left at the end of the month to even think of starting to save for a down payment. Timing is also a major factor in being able to buy your first home or move to another home. My wife and I were lucky to be able to buy a home in the same neighbourhood that we grew up in, and that had to do a lot with the state of the economy, mortgage rates, and stages of our careers to make everything fall into place.

"Home buying has been a mixed emotion topic for me. I come from a generation and live in a geographic area where my parents easily afforded a home on one income in the city when I was a child, but now I can only afford a modest condo in the suburbs even though my annual salary is much larger than my father's ever was. My advice to all single people is to buy as early as you can afford it. You can always rent out or sell if your life circumstances change. With retirement saving, the earlier you start the earlier you can finish, and the same holds true with getting and paying off your mortgage." – Lisa

"Try to minimize the amount of rent you have to pay. Investing into a home that you pay a monthly mortgage is an investment...you will never be able to re-coup the money you put into rent." - Diane

Importance of Insurance (Life, Critical Illness, Disability, Group Benefits)

When it comes to discussing different types of insurance needs, I believe it is better to be informed about the options and have the chance to say no rather than wish you had that discussion with your financial planner after it's too late.

"As a single person with no dependents, life insurance isn't a high priority for me. I have basic coverage at my workplace which is sufficient. I have some coverage (critical illness) at my workplace. I think it is important for single people to have some basic coverage for this eventuality, to ensure you can still pay bills and take care of yourself. It is also one of many reasons to have an emergency fund in place. I am fortunate to work for an excellent employer that provides extensive coverage, so I have found the various insurance plans I have through work sufficient." – Lisa

Not nearly as important as critical illness and disability coverage.
- Wendy

"An unexpected injury left me no choice but to go on short term disability, which I thankfully had through my employer's group benefit plan. Through that phase of my life, I came to realize the importance of ensuring that I have a plan in place for the unexpected injury or illness. As a single gal with no children, I have determined that life insurance is not nearly as important as critical illness and disability coverage. Nor do I wish to rely on a group benefit plan as our jobs can also have unexpected turnarounds. I feel more secure knowing I have critical illness coverage. If something happens, I hope to be in a position to continue to take care of myself financially. It doesn't feel good to wonder if you should be selling your car while recovering from an injury or an illness or asking for assistance from your family." – Wendy

"Life insurance hasn't been a major financial driver as I have no children, but critical (illness) insurance is important, especially as I am self-employed." - Diane

Financial Advice for Single People

Just like two married couples could react to financial advice differently, so do the views of single people. It comes down to goals, desired lifestyle, and knowing that you have to look after today first so that you will be able to look after tomorrow. It is one's interpretation of financial advice that keeps your financial planner on his or her toes (or should).

"Financial advice to single people: set some goals for yourself and you will be amazed how you can achieve them. Mine were around buying my own home and then being mortgage-free by the age of 40, and I focused my finances around those goals and achieved them. And, always max out your RRSPs every year, as soon and as early as you can in your life...it is the best way to start building a large savings fund that can start making money for you." - Diane

"For women in particular, I'd like to say even if you plan to get married and have children, it is best to act financially as if you were single until those happy events happen. You can't be sure where your life is going to lead; don't put off buying a home and saving for emergencies or retirement until you are older or married. The reality is today is when you have more disposable income, so put the money aside now. You'll just be in better financial shape when you do decide to get married and have a family. And if you do wind up living a single life, you'll be in good shape financially. Whatever may happen in your life, you want the ability to take care of yourself." - Lisa

Will, Estate Planning, and Beneficiary Decisions

Whether you are single or not, I believe that each one of us works hard and deserves the standard of living we desire. It is of great comfort to know that if something happens to us and we lose our ability to maintain our desired standard of living, a plan is in place to fulfill our wishes.

Will, estate planning, and beneficiary decisions are all based around death or injury, and it is not an easy topic to discuss. I know when my wife and I completed our will, powers of attorney, and beneficiary decisions; I was glad that it wouldn't come up again for me personally until something had to be changed. If you don't have this done, PLEASE make it a priority!

> *Having a will and estate planning with beneficiary decisions is important.*
> - **Diane**

"Having a will and estate planning with beneficiary decisions is important as a single person to ensure my assets are properly allocated to my family and friends if something unexpected happens." - Diane

"This (will) is something I seem to perpetually put off, though I know it is important. I imagine if I had dependents it would be a higher priority. Though I do not want to leave a probate mess behind when I pass away either, particularly if I die before my last surviving parent does. Right now the beneficiary decision has been easy as I am single; my mother is the primary beneficiary named on all my financial instruments. I have an elderly aunt, who I could leave money to, but no sisters/brothers or nieces/nephews. If my mother dies before

I do, I will likely name friends and the children of friends."
– Lisa

Other Advice

"My only other advice would be financial advice I'm sure you've heard in other places: live below your means, don't accumulate consumer debt, always put aside money for retirement and emergencies, and buy a home and pay it off early if you can." – Lisa

"It's hard when we want to be out and about, wining and dining, socializing, exercising, joining clubs, buying pretty clothes—sometimes we just can't do it all and need to accept financial changes." – Wendy

I hope that hearing views from three single Canadians confirmed that you are thinking the same way, created some questions to ask your financial planner at your next meeting, or gave you the courage to create that financial planning to-do list that will be completed very soon.

Sharper Focus

- Make an appointment with a legal professional to create or update your will. Make sure that your wishes will be followed through with, whether you pass away or can't make decisions for yourself going forward.

- Phone up a single friend of yours to schedule a coffee time together to discuss what is important to you.

- Speak with your parents about how they handled finances when they were single.

CHAPTER 53

Marriage and Money

Marriage orients men and women toward the future, asking them not just to commit to each other but to plan, to earn, to save, and to devote themselves to advancing their children's prospects. - **Daniel Patrick Moynihan**

Initiating
Conversations

Did you and your spouse go through money management counselling prior to getting married?

Did your spending and saving habits change once you got married?

If you have children, what spending and saving habits have changed?

My grandparents were married in 1945. Like the quote above, they have truly devoted themselves to their children's prospects and have continued to do so with their grandchildren and great grandchildren. As a parent myself, I know from experience that something in your brain switches once you have children. I realize now that it is my job to provide my kids with resources and wisdom that will enable them to get a good start in life, adulthood, and beyond.

My wife Wendy and I were married August 2, 1998 (I will keep this page marked so that I will forever remember) and as a financial planner, I know firsthand that marriage doesn't automatically create a combined view in regards to money. Marriage creates a need to develop and decide on a family money view that combines different backgrounds, traditions, and beliefs into one 'our money view'. Your *No, didn't have much, but know that it would have been a good idea given what we know now.* money view will change throughout your lifetimes so the sooner the better to create your first definition of your family view.

Your family view on money will continue to be a work in progress, and therefore regular meetings are a must outside of your regular meetings

with your financial planner. Whether it is just reviewing your budget or setting a goal for a big purchase,
you and your spouse or partner should set up a regular time to discuss your combined money management. This schedule should be more frequent in the
beginning and then monthly or quarterly once you
are both on the same page. If things start to get off
track, you should go back to more frequent discussions until your family money definition is solid.

*Yes, we have
had to create
a plan together
rather than two
separate plans
with a common
goal in mind.*

I have to admit that I am more of a spender and my wife is more of a
saver. Each of us came from different family views about money, which
has benefited us tremendously as a family. With our busy schedules, we
soon came to a compromise that Wendy would become our family CFO
(Chief Family Officer) even though I am a financial planner. An unpaid
position, but it has the very important title of 'Money Boss'. In order to
maintain our family standard of living and to meet the goals we have
for our family, we both work full-time. This is much different from when
I grew up, where only my father worked full-time, as my mom already
had the full-time position of 'Domestic Engineer', in which she worked
many over-time hours.

Financial planning discussions in a marriage encompass almost every aspect of a financial plan, as you bring your individual cash flow, budget,
and net worth statements together to create a new combined statement. . (There are exceptions to the rule with second marriages and beyond due to estate planning reasons.) Here are some financial planning
discussions that you should have before or early on in your marriage:

Bank accounts – Should you have separate or joint bank accounts?
It depends. Some couples like to set an amount that each spouse con-
tributes to the family account and then keep the remaining balances
in their own separate accounts. Other couples put all their money into
one pot and take an agreed amount out for personal expenses. Still yet,
others keep separate accounts and divide the different fixed and variable expenses up. In the end, as long as you meet your monthly cash

flow needs, contribute enough for your retirement, and are happy, then that's the way to go. If it doesn't work, then try another way.

Family history of money – Spouses will often come from different backgrounds where money and finances are viewed differently. One spouse could be a spender and the other a saver. Or, one spouse could come from a family when times were always spent living paycheque to paycheque, while the other spouse comes from a family that didn't have any money issues at all. Finding a common definition of how you would like your family money legacy to be remembered by your children is the best way to go.

Saving for your children's future – Your personal financial experience for your own education can weigh on the decisions you make for your own children's educations. One spouse could have had their first year of school paid for while the other spouse could have had to borrow money for their first year tuition. My family goal is that my wife and I would like to have our children have the money needed to attend one year of post secondary education (with an RESP and other savings) so that they will go to school right away (I had trouble focusing on school after a year away after graduating high school) and then have enough in our family financial plan (it will help if we have already paid off our mortgage and have no other debts) to have the assets to pay for the rest of their school costs or be able to provide for other purposes (i.e. down payment for a home) if our children do not continue their studies.

Investing and risk – After the wedding is over and you are getting settled into a happy marriage, you will have to make different decisions together about different life events before or as they occur. One of the first life events may be buying your first home. You will need to come to a mutual decision on the amount of money you can afford to borrow and what risk or debt you are willing to take on. The decision between a fixed rate mortgage and a variable rate could create a difference of opinion, but a decision needs to be made. Investing could be another difference of opinion, as investment risk tolerances could be much different and could affect your overall retirement plan if the risk and returns aren't reviewed on a regular basis.

Conflict – Money stress is one of the main causes in divorce. It might not seem like a big deal during the early years of your marriage, but if each spouse is not open and honest with each other, then there could be a snowball effect that gets out of control quickly. Often spending habits and consumer debt are two big problems that can be fixed if discussed

Things I have wanted in the past became a low priority once our children were born.

in the beginning, but the discussion is often left until it is too late. The bank account decision (joint vs. separate accounts) could be a catalyst to this issue, but in the end, discussions on a regular basis to see how 'our' finances are doing can go a long way. This is why pre-marriage financial planning classes are valuable if offered. I recommend that everyone go through these classes even if you believe that you have all the answers.

Will and power of attorney – It is absolutely important to review and update your will and power of attorney's. In a situation where you may have different beliefs, it is important to create wills and power of attorneys to make each other's goals met and compromise on a few parts if necessary. Even if you don't have any children or many assets, you should still have wills and power of attorneys completed through your lawyer or notary. This will ensure that each of you understand what is to happen if the other were to die or become physically unable to care for themselves. Or, if you were both to die in a common accident, the estate will be looked after as you wanted.

It is important to have the discussions above so that this doesn't happen:

Debt cheating – A small little one-time purchase without your spouse knowing doesn't seem like a big deal, as you may chalk it up to being part of 'my spending / no questions asked money that I am allowed to have'. But, if things start to get out of control with debt, it can only be hidden for so long before your credit rating is downgraded and the other sources for borrowed money dry up. This can also affect the credit of your spouse if you start to rack up joint credit cards that only you see the statements for.

Tina Tessina, psychotherapist and author of *Money, Sex, and Kids: Stop Fighting about the Three Things That Can Ruin Your Marriage* believes that, "Betrayal regarding money can be just as painful and damaging as other kinds of cheating," and the relationship can create a "total loss of trust, feelings of betrayal and destruction of the relationship."[1]

Boston-based family therapist Carleton Kendrick says, "The chief reasons people lie about money to their partners are pragmatism, control, guilt and fear. The pragmatic lie may result from planning an eventual split and not wanting the other to know how much money is available. Financial infidelity for control may include revenge spending, as one partner overspends to prove their independence or to get back at the other for something lacking in the relationship. Knowingly irresponsible behavior may cause guilt and embarrassment, so the person attempts to cover it up. Deceit may also occur because they fear their partner's reaction to the truth."[2]

If you do your best to communicate together about your family financial plan and don't get caught in any negative money behaviours, you will be rewarded by getting to where you want to be in the near and distance future. As you meet your goals, make sure that you budget in a 'date night' as those will be few and far between as your lives together get busier than they were before you tied the knot.

---

[1] Jenna Goudreau. 'Is your partner cheating on you financially' Forbes online Jan 13.2011.

[2] http://www.forbes.com/sites/jennagoudreau/2011/01/13/is-your-partner-cheating-on-you-financially-31-admit-money-deception-infidelity-red-flags-money-lies/2/

Sharper

- Ask your parent's how they created their own 'money view' when they were married.
- Ask your friends about how they developed their money view
- How have you overcome obstacles in the past that has affected your money view?

CHAPTER 54

Divorce and Starting Over

Divorce is the one human tragedy that reduces everything to cash. - **Rita Mae Brown**

Initiating Conversations

If you have children from a previous marriage, is it important to you that they receive your assets when you die?

What is the best way to decide how to split assets and liabilities when you are proceeding to a divorce?

How can I be financially stable now that I am single again?

This is where you need to take full control of your financial well-being. If you have left your family finances up to your spouse or partner, you need to stop and start to learn what you need to know to prepare yourself for what you face in the near future.

When it comes to going your separate ways after an unsuccessful marriage, most decisions are made based on the current and future value of assets and other responsibilities that often have a price attached (spousal and child support). Emotion will become an influence on your thoughts that can create decisions that may hurt you in the future. Feeling that you just want this done and be able to move on may seem like the easiest way in the 'heat of the battle', but you have to remember that you have to look out for #1 and any dependants that you may have.

Where marriage creates a need for two separate financial plans to become a single

Yes, you may want the income from your assets going to your new spouse. But upon his or her passing, you most likely want all assets to go to your children and not your second spouse's children. Things change if you and your second spouse have children together.

family one, divorce creates the opposite need. Once the divorce is official, you will need to create a brand new financial plan for yourself. You will realize that equal doesn't always mean 50/50 when current and future taxation is taken into consideration. Once everything is over with, you will be glad that you had all the information on the table so that you will come out of the divorce proceedings with what you feel is fair or as fair as it was going to get.

Steps to Take When You Know that Divorce is the Only Option

Know the official date of separation – You and your spouse need to agree on a date of separation as this will be important when you decide to apply for a divorce decree as well as deciding on asset and debt division.[1]

Gather all the financial data that you know about. This can include current bank statements, investment statements, list of liabilities (credit cards, mortgage statement), pension statements, and tax information.

Make a few phone calls. Contact the institutions that issued you credit in your individual name and joint names. It is always good to know what your credit balance is on a monthly basis on your personal and joint accounts. You will also want to make sure that you put a stop on all automatic authorizations on any joint banking and line-of-credit accounts, as assurance against potential malicious spending. Find out from your lender how to close any unnecessary accounts, or at least request the requirement to have both signatures for any future withdrawals. You need to protect your credit rating as much as possible. Although marriage is supposed to be built on trust, it may be a good idea to contact a credit agency to pull your credit report to make sure there are no credit cards taken out without your knowledge (individual or joint), as you can never be too careful.

---

[1] Divorce Dollars: Get your fair share: Financial planning before, during and after divorce. Akeela Davis – Sel Counsel Press 2009

Start to keep close track of expenses. It would be a good idea to start keeping track of all the expenses that you personally continue to pay for or now have to pay for due to the pending divorce proceedings. You want to make sure that you get credit for all expenses that you may have to cover in order to support your ex-spouse or kids that you believe your ex should be contributing to, but is not. If you need to continue to have a joint account, make sure you keep track of every last penny that is deposited or withdrawn.

The best way you see fit outside of legal requirements, but it may depend on how you both get along during the negotiations.

Negotiation

Do you need legal representation? Yes. It would also be valuable to have a financial planner with divorce experience and knowledge as part of your team. Not all lawyers are experienced or knowledgeable in financial planning divisions and future worth of assets, income, and the tax consequences that are affected depending on the decisions made. The financial planner with this unique knowledge can put together financial assumptions for you to take to review with your lawyer.

There are a number of different types of divorce proceedings. You will need to determine with your legal counsel what option will best suit your desired outcome and stress level. Please refer to the book website www.financialfotographs.com for examples of different divorce proceedings.

The Benefits of a Financial Planner with Expertise and Education in Divorce Settlements

During your marriage, you and your spouse may have used the same financial planner, so you both may not want to have him or her be part of the divorce proceedings. That is your call for any potential conflicts of interest. You should look for a financial planner with the desired experience to assist with the following:

Net worth statement – It is important to define your current net worth to assist in establishing market values on the date of separation or any other necessary date. Once these values are established then you can put together asset splitting proposals as you work towards an equitable split of all assets based on future growth and tax liabilities. For example, you may want to keep the house and give up pension splitting options or vice versa. Exhaust all possibilities so you know what you need to give in order to take what you want.

Cash flow statement – Your monthly cash flow will change once you decide on separation. Depending on your family situation (i.e. dependants, desire to go back to school, etc.) you will need to compare desired monthly and yearly cash flow statements and tax situations. If you are sacrificing income today for a benefit during retirement or if you and your spouse are going to split pension income you will want to know what the net effect will be and not just before taxes are taken off. The numbers on paper and the actual amount you get in your pocket after taxes could be significantly different.

Splitting of assets – You need to make sure you calculate reasonable growth rates for your house value, investments and other assets so that you know the effects of the decisions made during the divorce agreement and how they will look in the future or at retirement depending on how long your agreement will last.

Splitting of pensions – You will need to get the advice of an actuary so that you understand what options you have, as a 50/50 pension split could affect other asset division decisions that you make (e.g. keeping the family home, non-registered assets). You need to know the current and future values of any pensions so you can decide if you should take your pension portion now or during retirement depending on what negotiations take place and what the tax implications are.

Dependant costs – Outside of any legal rulings the division of costs for any dependants that you have is important to discuss and decide upon as this will affect your monthly cash flow, especially if you and your spouse don't agree to a division of these costs.

Insurance coverage –Having responsibilities in the divorce agreement regarding support (e.g. Child and spousal) should require guarantees that the obligations of support will continue if the party responsible becomes unable to fulfill the agreement due to disability or death. You could look to life insurance to cover this need. This should be brought up in discussions with your lawyer.

Although necessary, starting over will not be an easy task and you will need the support of others to assist where needed. Here are a few important tasks that should be done as soon as possible:

Create a financial plan that is 'you'. You may feel a need to be more conservative than you have been in the past. The best solution is to do what makes you comfortable and adjust from there.

Financial planner – Whether you stay with the same financial planner you had during your marriage or decide to seek a new one, it is important you take advantage of your chosen financial planner's services, network of other professionals and expertise, so that you are not alone starting over.

Estate plan, will, and power of attorney – One of the first things you should do is to speak with your lawyer or notary to see what changes need to be made to your will and power of attorney in order to ensure that your independent wishes are granted. You don't plan for something to happen, but you need to do this for peace of mind in the event that something does.

Budget – It is important to implement a reasonable budget that fits your new life situation. The budget may require a few adjustments before you are completely comfortable with it. It totally depends on the family structure that you have (e.g. your children live with you full-time or part-time). You also need to establish your own emergency fund that should be at least three times your monthly salary. It may not be the easiest to attain right away but you need to work towards it.

Standard of living – You will need to look at solutions to maintain your new standard of living so that money is available if you are unable to work for a period of time. This could complement any employee benefits you get at work. It is important to review, especially if you have been used to being part of your ex-spouse's benefit package.

Investments and risk tolerance – Once you know your portion of the division of assets, it is important to re-visit your investment portfolio and risk tolerance so your portfolios are re-balanced accordingly.

Financial plan – You will need to work with your financial planner on your new financial plan. You will have to go back to the beginning again and plan your future accordingly. Update your plan as often as needed.

Sharper Focus

- If you know of someone who has gone through a divorce, find out if it would be appropriate to have a discussion to find out any advice that you can gather. Maybe there is an advisor or two that they can recommend to you.

- Search for directories of advisors in your area that can assist you in your divorce needs.

- Find a family member or friend that can assist you in getting documents and other necessary information together.

CHAPTER 55

One of the Biggest Purchases You Will Ever Make!

You helped me buy my house! - **Brian Colledge**

Initiating
Conversations

Is it better to rent or buy a home?

How much should you save for your first home?

If you know that you will need to downsize during retirement, should you sell your home or is there a better idea?

When Brian thanked me for helping him buy his first home, I was confused. For the life of me, I did not know what he meant. I didn't give him any money, so I had to ask him what he was referring to. Brian explained to me that through the work that we did together saving for a down payment, I had helped him buy his home. I was honored to be able to help a client meet a goal, and for him to say thanks reinforced the reason why I enjoy being a financial planner.

Outside of the required down payment rules, you should put together scenarios that will show you how different down payment amounts will affect the interest savings over the lifetime of your mortgage versus the rent that you are paying.

I am sure that most Canadians have the dream of owning their home, but it is not as easy as you may think. You need to plan ahead and have confidence that once you buy your home, you will be able to afford all the expenses involved today, tomorrow, and further into the future. The last thing you want to do is jump into a home situation without doing all of your homework first.

To buy your home, you need to devise a strategy on how to come up with the required (or desired) down payment and then find a home that you can afford (which may be different from the home you want). You need to not only afford the home, but everything involved with owning it (i.e. taxes, insurance, and upkeep). In regards to applying for a mortgage, there can be a big difference between what you qualify for and what you can afford in the end.

Recommended Steps for Finding Your Home

Are you ready?

Most of the activities involved with buying a home are similar whether it is your first home, second, or beyond. Your needs and the numbers could be different which basically comes down to the fact that you may not be able to afford what you think you need. The first question you have to ask yourself is, "Am I ready?" Being ready is more than just saying "yes" because this type of purchase could become the biggest that you are going to undertake in your life.

Qualify for a mortgage

Other than on the rare occasion that you have enough equity built up to buy your home with cash you will need to qualify for a mortgage. This will most likely be the biggest source of debt that you will encounter; good debt, in my opinion, strictly because the equity growth within your personal residence is tax free.

Working with a mortgage broker will assist you in searching the marketplace for the best mortgage for you. Price is not 100% of the solution, as you need to find a mortgage that best suits you today and down the road. The rate that you will choose (variable or fixed), the term (5, 7, or 10 years) and the re-payment options will affect

It all depends on what your financial planning goals are today and what your budget will look like in the future.

your mortgage decision. Your mortgage broker will also assist you with every step of the mortgage application process which is more than just finding a mortgage.

Review your current and future budget with your financial planner

Once you have qualified for your mortgage, it is wise to meet with your financial planner to review how your future mortgage will affect your current monthly budget. You could find that you can qualify for a mortgage that is higher than you can afford and therefore your budget needs to be reviewed. It is vital to discuss all the new costs (fixed and variable) that will be included when your home purchase is final. The numbers could change as the house search progresses, so it's important to know the real numbers that you can work with. You don't want to go through the process of finding a home that you feel is 'the one' and then realize that you can't afford it once all the numbers are crunched. Just wasted stress in my opinion.

Find your dream home with your realtor

Once you are armed with the mortgage numbers and a budget that you feel comfortable with, the next step is to find a realtor. Just like when you are searching for a financial planner, it is beneficial to find a realtor that you are able to work well with, as this is an exciting time and often stressful even if you are prepared.

Keep in touch with your financial planner

In case any alterations need to be made in your homeowner budget, you will benefit by keeping in touch with your financial planner. An updated budget discussion may be necessary to see where spending can be cut (most likely variable expenses) if you need extra money to go towards the down payment or mortgage in order to get the home you really want.

Find a home inspector

Having a home inspector as part of your home buying team is critical that you know everything possible about the home you are going to buy. Knowing as many details as possible about your potential new home will assist you in putting together an offer with your realtor. The inspection will hopefully identify any extra costs that you may need to cover after you move in (which will affect your budget and offer), or you may find something that will make you decide to move on to another potential home.

Assemble the rest of your professional team to assist you in the purchase finalization

Once you have found your home, it is good to know the other professionals (i.e. lawyer or notary) you will need to find to finalize your purchase. I have found that your mortgage broker will be a great source for this as he or she will likely have a team to refer if you don't find your own.

Contact your financial planner when the final purchase goes through

It depends. If you want to keep your home then a change in your retirement standard of living will need to be adjusted.

Once you have officially purchased your home, it is important to provide your financial planner with the final numbers to be entered into your monthly budget. Make sure you pass along your annual mortgage statement to your financial planner so that everyone is kept up to date. Paying down your mortgage should be a high priority, so it is vital to develop strategies with your planner to pay down your mortgage sooner—within the rules of your particular mortgage. Don't be a stranger to your mortgage broker as keeping in contact will make sure that your mortgage rate and term is the best at all times rather than waiting to talk only when your mortgage comes due in the future.

One of the most frequent sources used by many first time homebuyers for the necessary down payment is their RSPs by using the Home Buyer's Plan (HBP). The most recent government forms and rules for the HBP are posted on the resource page at www.financialfotographs.com.

Sharper Focus

- Ask your parents or grandparents about how they saved for their first home and what their buying experience was like.
- Contact a mortgage broker to see what kind of mortgage you can qualify for. Can you afford it?
- Set up a meeting with your financial planner to see what amount of mortgage payments you could fit into your current budget.

CHAPTER 56

Are You Going to Be a Doctor, Wendy?

An investment in knowledge pays the best interest.
– Benjamin Franklin

Initiating
Conversations

Do you believe education will get you a better job for better pay?

Do you like the idea of borrowing funds from your retirement plan to further your education?

I sat in the audience of the convocation ceremony for my wife's last year in school (so she tells me) as she received her Master of Education degree from Simon Fraser University. It seems like such a simple ceremony for the many hours spent in study and class to attain her accomplishment. You know what I mean if you have achieved the same.

If not for better pay, it may get you stability and advancement opportunities in the future.

As the ceremony started, it was hard to miss the people with the funny hats who were announced first for the accomplishment of attaining a doctorate in their studies. I guess it is only fitting that if you get a doctorate you should go first and top it off with a hat that only a select few can claim to own. An expensive hat for sure!

After the ceremony was over, with my dry humour that my family doesn't get most of the time, I asked my wife, "Are you going to be a doctor, Wendy?" My motto is 'nothing ventured, nothing gained', so I inquired accordingly and received a 'to be determined' response. I guess the hat will have to wait.

Both my wife and I have a goal of higher education. Wendy once said that further education is her GIC, her guarantee in her profession. To equate that to what a financial planner has to do to maintain his or her registrations and designations, it does guarantee their profession also. I truly believe that the more that you are educated in a subject, belief system, job, or investment plan, the more comfortable you will be in making the necessary decisions.

Learning is a lifelong exercise, and the Canadian government is helping eligible Canadians to further their education with the opportunity to participate in the Life Long Learning Plan. You may have been told that RSPs are only for retirement, but I believe that there are two instances that you can use the assets within your RSP to increase your net worth, income, or receive a promotion. These two instances are through the Life Long Learning Plan and the Home Buyer's Plan. You do lose the growth potential of the investments that you borrow from your plan, but often it is the last ditch effort to raise funds for something that you have decided to do. As long as it is for an 'asset appreciation' possibility I won't bother with hind sight.

Don't want to have to borrow, but I know that I have the funds in case I want to attain a higher level of education to forward my career.

Rules of the Lifelong Learning Plan (LLP)

As government programs evolve and changes can be made the information on program length, withdrawal rules and program re-payment guidelines are included on the resource section of www.financialfotographs.com

So, if you are thinking about pursing further education, you may want to consider the LLP as an option to help you meet your financial and personal planning goals. It is wise to plan for this as far ahead as possible so that the original contributions inside your RSP are credited during the appropriate tax year(s) to get the best tax benefit available. Just as important, the investment portfolio that you choose within your RSP prior to participating in the LLP should meet the risk tolerance you are willing to take within the given timeline prior to withdrawal. This is important so that you have the amounts needed without having to borrow from other sources if the market is going through uncomfortable volatility when you need the money.

Sharper

Focus

- Ask an older friend or family member that went back to school later in life if they felt it was worth the time.

- If you are planning on going back to school do you know if this will enable you to increase your salary or if it will be an accomplishment you would like to attain?

- If you utilize the LLP plan ahead to make sure you will be able to pay it back within the government guidelines.

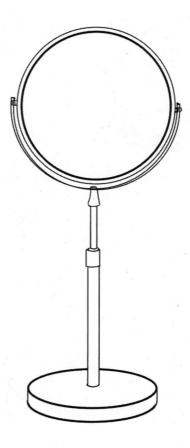

CHAPTER 57

My Art of Balance

What I dream of is an art of balance.
- Henri Matisse (1869-1954)

Initiating
Conversations

Would you follow your financial plan if you felt that you were tied to it every day?

Would you reward yourself if you met a financial planning goal?

Would you be happy if you had to work longer because you have a more flexible financial plan?

This chapter is not about becoming selfish when it comes to financial planning. Instead, it is a reflection on how you should focus on the exercise of developing a financial plan that meets your standard of living today as well as the goals you have set for yourself and family in the future. The ultimate goal would be to retire and create a standard of living that you deserve, but there are many goals that need to be met along the way until you reach retirement. Sometimes an 'end' goal only happens when certain other goals are made, and the act of rewarding yourself upon meeting a goal or combination of goals is important to discuss with your family and financial planner.

I would try but it would be hard and I might give up.

Financial plans or budgets are not always easy to follow—especially if there is no end in sight or you don't see the benefits along the way. Many people live in the 'now' and deal with the future when it comes. A financial plan or budget is dealing with the 'now' so that you have more control on what your future holds. It's hard work, but it is necessary to create a standard of living that you and your family enjoy. You have to find an 'art of balance'.

> *Rewards big or small are important to keep the interest of your financial plan going.*

What is your 'art of balance'? Is it going on a vacation once a year? Is it spending money on those extra cable channels or going out for dinner once a week? Or are you leaving the balance part of the equation for retirement since you feel that you will be working as many years as you will be retired?

If you haven't defined your 'art of balance' what is keeping you from it? Are you so out of balance with your lifestyle and your financial plan or budget that you feel as though it is not worth it? Is it that you just haven't sat down with a financial planner before and spent time defining your 'art of balance'?

The definition of your 'art of balance' will change throughout your life. Whether you get married, have children, change jobs, increase or decrease your yearly earnings, retire, or any other life event, you will need to re-examine what your 'art of balance' is.

Unless I create rewards for myself, I know that it would be hard to follow my financial plan. As a financial planner I don't see myself entering the full retirement stage in my life as I love what I do. I see myself finding a person or two to gradually take over my business during the 'normal' retirement years, allowing me and my family to meet some important 'fun' goals as there is no end date of my working years set in stone. Many people have jobs that enable them to have a succession plan, but you have to plan accordingly if things go off course whether you can control the change or not.

What an 'art of balance' is not: Rewarding yourself at the expense of your financial future. If you start adding rewards to your financial planning or budget goals throughout your life you need to make sure it doesn't get out of control. You should not go into debt to reward yourself. If you include your reward into your monthly budget and financial plan, then you are on the right track. If you get off track, just make sure that you are able to catch it and correct it in time before anything gets out of hand.

There are a few things to keep in mind when including a reward system within your financial plan: a lower investment and retirement portfolio, a longer mortgage amortization, and a delayed ideal retirement date.

A lower investment and retirement portfolio – It has often been said that you can never have too much money, but depending on your spending (reward) habits, your investment and retirement portfolio may not be as big. You might be tempted to increase your desired risk tolerance to try and make up the difference, but this often creates a further shortfall if the market doesn't behave. The solution would be to adjust your standard of living or plan to work a few extra years remembering that the adjustment is due to your lifestyle decisions (that I hope were positive), not the extra risk and unwelcome volatility in the market.

Yes, as long as it wasn't because I took too much risk with my investments.

A longer mortgage amortization – Everyone's goal is to pay off their mortgage as soon as possible. Hopefully the only time that you would be increasing your mortgage would be because you are adding value to your existing house or moving to another home. However, if you are to implement important goals and a reward system within your financial plan, you should be willing to take a longer mortgage amortization if needed to accommodate your rewards. The only reason you would have a longer mortgage amortization would be because you won't have extra money to put against the principal each year as it is instead geared towards your desired standard of living.

Delayed ideal retirement date – If you are someone who likes to work hard and play hard or wants to have a standard of living that may need extra monthly cash flow, you may need to sacrifice your ideal retirement date to sometime later than desired. It is not a done deal that you will have to do this, but you need to be open to this happening.

So feel free to work hard and play hard, but remember to *spend smart* to maintain your *'art of balance'*.

Sharper

Focus

- Set a budget goal for the next month and decide what a reasonable reward would be.

- If you are not happy with your current financial plan, make plans to meet with your financial planner to discuss.

- Schedule some fun time this month for you and your family.

CHAPTER 58

Taking Financial Planning Conversations Forward

"Use a picture. It's worth a thousand words."
**Arthur Brisbane to the Syracuse Advertising
Men's Club, in March 1911**

Initiating
Conversations

What is the best way to learn about financial experiences?

What is the best way to know where all the money goes?

What is the best way to pass along your final wishes to your family?

The reason I wanted to write this book was to contribute to financial literacy. I wanted to create an opportunity for you and your family to initiate financial conversations by using pictures and real life stories. I hope that you can use this book as a tool to make small contributions to your unique family financial planning tradition. In the end, your financial plan is yours to follow; only you can make it happen.

Financial planning is not the easiest task to follow given all life's curve-balls that are thrown at us. Just like a coach prepares a team's game plan, I believe that it is important to have a financial plan in place so that you are prepared as much as possible for any unforeseen events that occur.

Financial conversations should never end. The scope of a financial conversation will change along with the times but it is always vital to you whether you are single, married, a parent or someone else in your family unit.

How can you take financial planning conversations forward?

Family values

Forming family and individual financial values is important; whether you are starting from scratch or passing along wisdom you have gained from others.

After reading this book, what did you find important to you right now? Did you find a couple areas where you need to improve on or even start from scratch? Do you have someone who you could work with on these goals you have set for yourself or your family?

Financial knowledge

As the world changes, so does the depth of financial knowledge that is out there to learn. To some knowledge is dangerous, but I disagree. Build your financial knowledge 'step by step' and learn more today than you knew yesterday.

Talk and ask questions of your family and friends.

Taking a course that is focused on financial literacy, reading a book that is from a financial layman's perspective or continuing to ask your financial advisor questions on decisions that are being made are three good places to start. Just make sure that the sources are reliable and that your questions are answered. Knowledge will help you be proactive as much as possible and reactive less often.

Financial planning processes

From a textbook perspective the financial planning process is six steps. But each step can be personalized to your unique situation and a personal timeline can be established to get things done according to your needs. The main issue is to create a financial plan if you don't have one and to update your financial plan on a regular basis to make sure that everything is kept up to date as much as possible. When are you going to create your first financial plan? When was the last time you reviewed your existing financial plan?

Preparing for life's financial events

There are financial events that will definitely happen and those that you plan for just in case. It is better to be prepared so that you can have the tools in place to have the

Create and follow a budget.

most favourable outcome as possible. Money is the source of funding your financial events and therefore it is important to have an investment exit strategy for those funds needed for a particular event. If that event doesn't happen then you set a new strategy. It's much better to have a strategy that is not needed than not having a strategy at all. Do you have a strategy for each one of your life's or your family life's financial events that are happening now or may happen in the future?

Valuing both time and money

We each plan to retire as soon as possible but often forget that we need assets to do this. If you were to retire today how long before you would need to go back to work? My goal is to have clients at retirement age continue to work if they want to rather than because they have to. The earlier you plan the better chance you have to be able to make any necessary changes. I know of people who have retired for a couple years and then went back to work because they are bored. Or they have found time in their retirement schedule to donate a few hours each month to a particular hobby or charitable organization that is important to them. Have you had someone tell you before that they are busier in retirement than they were during their working years? What is important to you today that you may want to contribute to by way of money or time when you are retired?

Building harmonious family legacies

The most important part of any financial plan is making sure you have an updated will and power of attorney. Without getting into the legal aspect of a will it is a document that allows you to establish your legacy. It tells your family and friends how you want to leave this world and how you want your memory to live on. When it is time to decide what is best for you there is always the chance that you won't be in sound mind to be able to make that decision for you. If you don't have a will, then the government will be left to make decisions for you. So, do you have a will? If not, please GET ONE DONE! If you do have a will, does it need to be updated or reviewed?

Update your will and power of attorney.

Thinking about how you want to be remembered may seem slightly selfish to some, but I think it is important that wisdom gained from a life lived is very important to pass along to those that you love whether during your lifetime or after you have passed.

When I am near the end of my life on earth I would prefer to remember the memories of passing along my wisdom to others and watching my loved ones enjoy a part of the fruits of my labour rather than waiting for them to enjoy it once I am gone.

So the next time you look at a picture maybe it won't create a conversation of a thousand words, but hopefully a few words of either passing along financial wisdom to others or building upon your own financial wisdom by listening to others.

Sharper Focus

- Ask your parent's or grandparent's what kind of financial wisdom they can pass down to you.

- Ask your children what money means to them.

- Write down 5 activities that you need to do right now to create or update a financial plan that will meet everything that is important to you and your family today and into the future.